FIND YOUR WINGS AND FLY

A SEEKER'S JOURNEY AROUND THE WORLD

NIGEL SHAMASH

ARNICA PRESS

Published by ARNICA PRESS

www.ArnicaPress.com

Arnica Press is committed to publishing works of quality and integrity. In that spirit, we are proud to offer this book to our readers; however, the story, the experiences, and the words are the author's alone.

FIND YOUR WINGS AND FLY

A SEEKER'S JOURNEY AROUND THE WORLD

NIGEL SHAMASH

For my Mother and Father
for my three elder Brothers
and for Sally...

TABLE OF CONTENTS

INTRODUCTION

Corona, My Best Friend

I'm sitting on a beach in San Marcos by Lake Atitlan in Guatemala. The place is quieter than normal as most places are shut because of the Corona virus outbreak and it looks like I will be stuck here for a while. As I sit in the sun, listening to the waves gently lapping on the shore, I think to myself, what a wonderful place to be stuck!

Last night I looked across the lake and saw in the distance a volcano gently erupting. Yes, even the volcanoes are gentle here. This morning several of us in our little hotel took turns to lead a yoga breathing class. Tonight I will cook dinner for all six guests plus Santos, our Guatemalan host. I'm in my element here, even though I'm the only foreigner without piercings or tattoos. People smile and compliment me on my bright, colourful clothes and the women dance spontaneously when I play my guitar and play in the streets.

The locals call me *abuelo* (grandfather) which I found difficult at first, but I realize it's a sign of respect and I'm feeling happy being an elder. One of the great things about being older, and I'm 73, is that I care less and less about the opinions of others and I can be myself.

I'm on a sort of mission to bring colour into the world and spread love and laughter. I laugh at my face in the mirror in the morning and I run free laughter classes wherever I go.

I came here a couple of months ago to tour around Guatemala with a shaman, visiting sacred sites and learning about Mayan theology. And I so loved the place that I decided to stay longer. Now that the world is in crisis, I am no longer able to go back to France where I live. I've called this chapter "Corona, My Best Friend" because it has forced me to stay in this beautiful country and take time to write my story. There is another reason why I call it my "friend". The shaman conducting the course that I attended here explained that in the Mayan calendar which was formulated about 2500 years ago, 2012 marked the end of a 26,000 cycle. The new cycle which would start in 2030 would augur happier times. This year 2020 was in the middle of the transition period, what the Mayans call "no time" and we could expect dramatic events in 2020. This was in January, before the Corona virus took hold and caused such chaos in the world.

In spite of all the deaths and financial hardships, I choose to see the virus as a friend, as something positive, the harbinger of the changes that I have been praying for these past forty-five years.

At San Marcos, next to Lake Atitlan, Guatemala

I have had an eventful life. I was born the fourth son of Jews from Baghdad in Iraq and we grew up outside an isolated village in Scotland, the only Jews in the village. After my university studies and a banking career in Argentina I had some life changing moments in my mid 20's when I discovered yoga. My story recounts my travels all over the world, living in communities and studying with gurus, some of them well-known, others less so. It chronicles my disillusionment with gurus, leading to setting up a therapy centre called Cortijo Romero in Spain in the 1980's. I talk about my marriage with Rachel, my children and the heartbreak of Rachel leaving me for a mutual friend. I now have an alternative holiday centre near Toulouse and with my daughter Anna; we organize residential courses in English on themes such as yoga, music and dance. It's going to be closed for the foreseeable future since France has banned international travel and so I won't be hurrying home.

I can hear Reggae music in the background and everyone that walks by smiles and talks for a while. Writing this story has been a great gift to me, because it has enabled me to appreciate all the wonderful things which happened to me, even though they didn't always seem wonderful at the time. I realize that I often concentrated on the negative things that happened, the beatings from sadistic teachers at school for example, rather than the wonderful help and encouragement I received from family, friends and mentors throughout the years.

I think back over my life and remember how shy and insecure I was as a fifteen year old and realise what a long way I have come. These insecurities propelled me to a life of wondering and searching and from this I have developed more compassion and insight. I've always delayed writing my memoirs, because I thought I needed to be some sort of enlightened being with a cosmic message. But it is precisely because I am a work in progress that my life may be of interest to you, the reader.

Yes, I can still be anxious and insecure but I am more able to wave goodbye to these thoughts and come back to the present moment. I am an altogether happier and more fulfilled person with a better understanding of my purpose in life of inspiring people and helping to spread love and laughter.

This is the story about my life and the changes that I have been through.

ONE

THE ONLY JEW IN THE VILLAGE

My parents were Jews from Baghdad who arrived in rural Scotland in 1939 to start a business and a family. I was part of that family, the youngest of four boys, born in 1947. I've often had recurring dreams throughout the years and these usually concern my early years in Scotland. When I can't remember a dream I usually go to the theme of playing golf. Why golf? My father was a passionate man and golf was his greatest passion. We were nominally Jewish and dad took this quite seriously but I always felt that golf was our true religion. Although not much of a golfer himself he was always pontificating about the inner workings of the game. He also realised that being a good golfer in Scotland was a great way to make friends and influence people. "Work hard and play hard, darling," he used to say and we four brothers took the game very seriously.

Our spare time was spent on the golf course, always dreaming of winning some major championship. Occasionally golf professionals would come to stay and teach us and we played in golf tournaments all over the country.

Before a big game dad would always get us to say our prayers in Hebrew and he would continue, "Remember darling, it's only a game." Huh, I thought, not true! I was a very good golfer for my age. When I was twelve I got round our local course in 70 (if that means anything to you).

My oldest brother Edward was even better and achieved a great deal of success at the national level.

At the age of about fifteen the hormones kicked in strongly and I started thinking non-stop about girls. Golf became less important. Dad was getting old by then and he had a bit of a wake-up call when he realised we should be studying more and playing less golf.

As my older brothers left home to go to university I longed desperately to join them and I spent a year working extremely hard to go to university a year earlier than was normal. This is another of my recurring dreams. I'm having to study for exams or I'm late for exams or I have to take my exams again.

My parents were part of a big Jewish community from Baghdad who came to settle in West Didsbury, Manchester in the early part of the 20th century. They mostly exported printed textiles made in Lancashire to Iraq and other parts of the world.

THE FOUR SHAMASH BROTHERS FROM KIRKCUDBRIGHT, SCOTLAND, WHO PLAYF · IN THE CARRIS TROPHY AT MOOR PARK. *(Left to right)* EDWARD (17), DONALD (15), ALAN (14), NIGEL (11)

Four Golfers, with my brothers in 1959.
Left to right, Edward, Donald, Alan and Nigel.

My father Maurice was a successful business man and quite a visionary. He got married to my mother Habu in 1939 just before the outbreak of the Second World War. Fearing large-scale bombardment from the Germans he bought a bankrupt silk factory and a house in rural Scotland and moved there to start a family.

This was a brave move because life in Scotland was alien to anything my parents had known before. As an aside, when I think of all the bomb sites that were still dotted all over Manchester in the 1950's, he made a good move.

He sold the machinery in the factory for a good profit and decided to go into the egg business. Off he goes to market without the least bit of knowledge about hens. He ended up buying a huge flock of cocks and was very relieved when a local farmer, realising that he was clueless, took them off his hands. He learned quickly and eventually he had 150,000 hens laying eggs and 20 or so workers. I never liked the chicken factory, the smell, the noise, the flapping of the wings and it perhaps explains why I became a vegetarian at a young age. He continued his cotton exporting business in Manchester and on weekends he would come home to supervise his poultry factory.

1939 Mum and Dad's wedding

We lived in a tiny village 2 miles from Kirkcudbright, a picturesque town near the sea, well loved by many artists because of the peculiar quality of the light.

I remember always feeling torn between two cultures. We were four boys living in the country and we had very few friends in the vicinity. We were encouraged to play together rather than make friends outside the family.

Consequently family life although mostly very happy, was also very intense. I worshiped my three elder brothers

Edward, Donald and Alan although I sometimes rebelled against their authority.

When I left the comfort of my family it was always very scary. I remember being inconsolable and crying incessantly during my first two days at school. Nothing made sense, my mother had taught me to read and write at the age of three and here we were playing with bricks and reciting nursery rhymes. And yet I wanted so much to fit in. I didn't want to be Jewish and have to sit on my own, excluded from Christian prayers. I love my family but I also wanted to be accepted and loved at school. Fortunately there was no anti-Semitism.

We were the only Jews in the village and most of the other children had no concept of what a Jew was. I remember Jimmy Swan asking me, "Nigel, are you a Protestant or Catholic?"

"Neither," I replied, "I'm a Jew."

"Aye," he went on, "but are you a Protestant Jew or a Catholic Jew?" I usually sided with the Protestants. They were in the majority and Catholics were seen as being a bit strange.

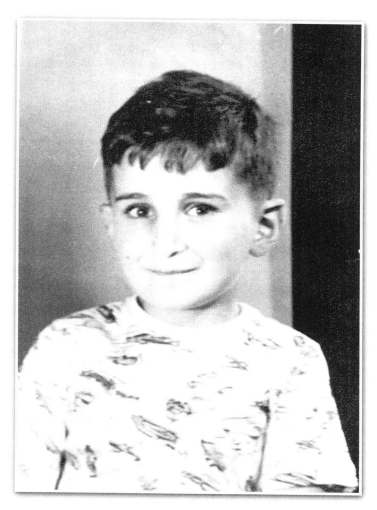

At age eight

School meals were a disaster. I was used to my mother's Middle Eastern cooking. She was a brilliant cook, always able to conjure up some exotic delicacy made with rice, meat and vegetables usually straight from the garden. This was a far cry from Scottish fare in the 1950's. The meals were very starchy and any vegetables served were soggy and overcooked. The specialty was dessert.

I remember that we had sugar rationing right up to 1953 but once rationing was stopped, the Scots took to it with a vengeance. Custard, cakes and all sorts of trifles and even the legendary fried Mars bar.

I really wanted to fit in with the other boys at school and play something other than golf and I was delighted when aged eleven, I was invited to play centre forward for the Kirkcudbright Junior Football team. Dad was equally enthusiastic, more than enthusiastic. He would run up and down the touchline, yelling in his thick Arabic accent, "Onto heem," darling. Of course I wanted to curl up and die. Nobody in Scotland called their children "darling" and nobody showed passion of any sorts except when drunk. A stiff upper lip was the order of the day. At halftime he would bring a big box of oranges for both teams; a kind gesture, but a mixed blessing as far as I was concerned. I remember a team mate saying, "Ach Shamash, ye'r only in the team because ye'r faither brings us oranges." This wasn't strictly true, I wasn't a great footballer but I think I was just about good enough to make the team.

The Scots in the 1950's were very anti-English. They remembered the wars of the past and in history lessons in school when we learned of the victories against the English of the Scottish heroes, William Wallace and Robert the Bruce we would all cheer and celebrate. Discipline at school was very strict, especially in secondary school. Some of the teachers were quite sadistic and regularly used corporal punishment. For me it was an enormous humiliation to be belted in front of my classmates, especially since my parents never laid a hand on me. I felt bad about those teachers but I have come to realise that that was how things were done at that time and they didn't know any better.

Outside the family and close friends I was painfully shy. Perhaps this was because of my rather authoritative father. I never really started to find my voice until I left home. I could also be anxious and obsessive. This obsessive behavior would surface from time to time whenever life was stressful. Obsession can be scary because it is so illogical, as if your thoughts become bigger than you. My left sock had to be higher than my right or I would obsess about the right meaning of some word. I remember my dad threatening to send me to a psychiatrist and thinking; yes, please do! But in those days children didn't confide in their parents or express their needs clearly. You did what you were told. I couldn't talk about my anxieties with my friends at school or my brothers either because I didn't really have the language to convey my feelings.

Most of the time though, I was happy and carefree. My mother was kind and loving and we all adored her. She devoted her life to her husband and four boys and was universally popular and respected. It was a lot of work looking after four boys in the days before washing machines. Luckily she had the help of a wonderful Scots woman Sally who lived with us. Sally had arrived in our family the year before I was born and I was always her favourite. In those days the nanny would sit in the kitchen whilst we as a family would sit rather formally in the dining room. I loved Sally and was sometimes allowed to sit with her while she ate. Her passions were music and dancing and she taught me lots of old Scottish folk songs. To her delight as a very young boy I would get up on a chair and sing to her.

We boys had a pact of conspiracy to avoid the eagle eyes of my dad and we would always be looking for ways to defy his authority. To avoid his strict curfew rules, I would stuff pillows and a football disguised as a head in my bed, make a very convincing show of being tired and would then slip out of the door unnoticed to go and play.

Scottish winters could be long, dark and cold and we boys would amuse ourselves playing card games, reading and listening to the radio. (TV was banned as it was considered, probably very wisely, a waste of time). Every Sunday evening my parents would have guests over to play bridge, either teachers from our school, local dignitaries or well heeled farmers. They would play in the guest room in the front of the house. We boys would play in the back of the house next to where the cars were parked. Mum would come by just once in the evening to bring the guests tea and cucumber and smoked salmon sandwiches, beautifully prepared with the crusts cut off, plus homemade meringues.

Sunday nights in winter seemed to drag on forever and I would get bored. Thirsty for adventure, I started taking our parents' cars out on the open road, using cushions to prop myself up so that I could see out of the windscreen. There were far fewer cars on the roads in those days and it didn't seem to matter that I couldn't manage to get into anything higher than second gear in those first few weeks. Borrowing cars is a bit like a drug for a bored young boy and little by little I taught myself how to use the gears properly. Luckily I never crashed a car although I had some near escapes and even more luckily I was never discovered by my parents.

Summers were never boring. We always had plenty to do; trees to climb, a rocky river to explore and best of all, visits from our Manchester cousins. My favourite cousins were the Yentob twins, Robert and Alan (who later became a leading figure with the BBC). I loved being part of a big extended family. We were about 15 cousins, more or less the same age and we were all like brothers and sisters to each other.

We would often go to Manchester in the school holidays and stay with our cousins the Yentobs. They had an enormous house in West Didsbury and they were usually up to 20 people in that house. Evenings the adults would get together to play bridge and poker. What a noise they made! It was so different from the British. I always thought there was some sort of argument going on but no, they were simply discussing the ins or outs of bridge or poker strategies.

On Saturdays we would go to the local West Didsbury synagogue. It was a Sephardic synagogue and they followed the traditions of the Mediterranean Jews as opposed to the Ashkenazim Jews who came from the north of Europe and spoke Yiddish. The Sephardic synagogue was very traditional. The women sat upstairs out of the way, always engaged in animated discussion.

The men down below did their fair share of talking, although there were one or two who seemed to take the prayers seriously, their heads bobbing up and down. I hated it. It was all in Hebrew which I could read but couldn't understand. When I looked at the translations of some of the prayers, they seemed nonsensical. I remember having to recite our prayers every Sunday (dad worked on Saturday, the traditional day for Jewish prayers) and we would say, "Blessed art thou, oh Lord our God, for not making me a woman." Even as a 12 year old I knew that this was nonsense. The only thing I liked was the singing and the harmonies. They seemed to make it up as they went along and it sounded great to my ears.

There were many things I loved about being Jewish. It was mostly about being part of a large, loving clan. Education was valued. We had books everywhere and all my cousins went to university. Music was highly regarded. I remember growing up with classical music in the background, especially if my mother was around. As a young boy I grew up with crooners such as Bing Crosby, Frank Sinatra and Dean Martin. When I first heard Elvis singing "King Creole" one evening, I felt an explosion of joy. I remember being in my bedroom and tearing down the stairs. It was so exciting, vibrant and different from anything I'd ever heard before.

The BBC only allowed 45 minutes of pop music per week as it was considered degenerate and many of the clergy of the day condemned it as being music of the Devil. We would listen to radio Luxembourg. Sunday night was Top of the Pops and I and so many of my school mates would listen from 11 pm till midnight. We had to stay listening right till the end because that was when they played the number one hit. In those days there was far less variety of music and we tended to all know the same songs. We were all passionate about music, especially with the advent of the Beatles, the Rolling Stones, The Kinks and The Who. If anyone ever had enough money to buy one of the vinyl records of the day it would be played and played until it would become cracked and useless. Even today I remember the words of almost all the hit songs of that period. I'm not saying it was all good music but a lot of it was original and has stood the test of time and many youngsters listen to modern covers of these songs without realising that they came from the 60's. My favourite music from my childhood was a version of Bizet's Carmen called Carmen Jones which is an Afro-American adaptation of the original and I can safely say that I know every single word of it.

The highlight of the year for me was always two or three weeks in a fancy hotel. In those days big 4 or 5 star hotels would offer their guests a package which included all meals, games and entertainment for all the children. My favourite one was the Palace Hotel in Torquay, Devon. Dad always chose a hotel with a golf course. The meals were often a seven course affair, the best part being the sweets trolley where we could choose from six or seven different types of desserts.

I look back on my childhood and have many happy memories. As a young man in my 20's, lost, unsettled and looking for answers, I turned to psychotherapy. At the time it was all about releasing childhood traumas, caused by parents. I remember my mother asking me once, "What did we do wrong?" I didn't know what to say. There was nothing I could put my finger on. I wish she were here now and I would tell her what an amazing mother she was to we boys and to all her nephews, nieces and grandchildren.

As for my father, when I was struggling to understand my insecurities and angst, I would blame him for his authoritative ways and his insistence that we'd excel at everything. However, I came to understand that he was born in a very different world from me. He was over 50 when I was born, and fathers in those days believed strongly that children needed discipline. I know that he loved us passionately and he worked extremely hard to give us a high standard of living which I tended to take for granted. He travelled from Scotland to Manchester every week to work on his export business and it was always very difficult for him to leave us. There were often tears in his eyes as he waved us goodbye.

TWO

SEXUAL AWAKENING

As a young boy, growing up in the 50's in the UK, sex was very much a taboo subject. Homosexuality was little understood and what's more, illegal. Everything was done behind closed doors.

I remember around the age of nine or ten, having fantasies that the woman who used to sweep the street outside her front door beside our school, would put me over her knee and smack me solidly. Other times I would stick my bottom out of the window, hoping the neighbour, Mrs Bramptom would see me. On another occasion I ran down the road naked. When I heard a neighbour, Mrs Marshall coming, I hid in an abandoned house and covered myself with leaves when she came to investigate what was going on. These fantasies were completely taboo and not to be shared even with my closest friends. I only learned about the sexual act aged 11 because I read about it in an article in the Encyclopaedia Britannica, a series of 26 large books. I loved those encyclopaedias and I remember gazing fondly at photos of Greek nude statues until my brother Donald caught me. Volume 20 of Encyclopaedia Britannica was henceforth hidden away.

I used to enjoy rubbing my penis up and down the bed sheets and then wonder of wonders, aged thirteen, I had an orgasm. From that day onwards it was mayhem. Never a day passed without masturbation. The mere thought of it would get me going. I remember thinking that if I ever became anxious or obsessive, I would just masturbate non-stop all day long. Fortunately I was able to talk about this with my friend Bruce. I had the beginnings of acne and he advised me that it was caused by masturbation. His reasoning was that we sweat when we masturbate and this exacerbates the acne. I wasn't sure whether this made sense but acne is a terrible affliction at that age and so I thought, what the heck, I'll give it a go. For 8 torturous days I abstained but the acne didn't go away. It even got worse and so it was back to business as usual.

It was very hard to come across pictures of naked women in those days but where there is a will there's a way and I managed to procure some through the post (always discreetly wrapped in brown paper). All seemed to be going well until the day I negligently left my pictures under the bed. Sally, our nanny discovered them and discretely removed them without saying a word to me.

Not so long afterwards, my dad came into my bedroom and started to tell me about how "playing with yourself" caused blindness. But I'd studied my

Encyclopaedia Britannica and I knew by then that this was nonsense and I was undeterred. (I can report that I am now 73 and don't wear glasses.)

Yes, sex was an obsession and yet I had very little contact with girls. For some reason it wasn't considered to be manly to hang out with girls and anyone caught doing so would be teased mercilessly. Little by little though, as I got older, I started to take tentative steps towards talking to girls. I used to walk home from school with Jocelyn and Jane. I was in love with Jocelyn at the time, one of several girls that I was in love with. I remember gazing at her and thinking that I would be prepared to cut off my right hand just to feel one of her breasts. Just a little side note: I met Jocelyn some 50 years later at a class reunion and told her the story and she replied, "Ach, Nigel, you should have just asked!"

And then I was fifteen and it was 1962, **The Year of the Kiss**. I was at the school dance and I had heard that Margaret Black liked me. However, it took until the very last dance to pluck up courage, to ask if I could walk her home. It was a freezing cold night but there was a full moon and I had my first kiss. My whole body tingled. I felt so alive. And that was even without using our tongues. We didn't know about tongues in those days.

And then came 1963 **The Year of the Tit**. Same procedure. I asked a girl called Wendy if I could walk her home and after a long and fond kiss, lying on the grass and groping around, I felt her tits. Nothing else was allowed but I did feel like I had passed some sort of milestone. Yes, I was on a mission. Later that year I was playing in a golf tournament in London and I took the train to Soho in Central London and went to a strip club. "Ah! Ah! Ah!" Endless inspiration for my fantasies. I used to wonder if other boys were as obsessed with sex as I was. I would occasionally talk about masturbation with my friends but it seemed to me that I was more highly sexed than anyone I knew. I remember being very relieved when I read Philip Roth's "Portnoy's Complaint" which chronicles the sex drive of a young man who seemed to be in a similar situation as myself.

And then came 1964, **The Year of the Screw**. I was in Estoril in Portugal just north of Lisbon with my parents and all my cousins. One hot sticky night I took the train into Lisbon and headed to the red light district. I went into a bar and, scared as hell but also highly excited, through a mixture of gestures and words, I hired the services of a prostitute.

Now Portugal in 1964 was ruled with an iron fist by Salazar, the dictator and prostitution was highly illegal. I remember a taxi ride with my newfound friend hiding under the seat to avoid the police. When the danger seemed to have passed, I tentatively stroked her leg and she responded by grabbing my penis and indicating that I keep my head down. I couldn't believe that anyone could be so brazen. It seemed so strange, abrupt and unromantic. No woman had ever taken the initiative like that before. We arrived in a rather downtrodden hotel room. I had no idea what to do. Remember, there was no pornography in those days. She undressed and proceeded to wash her vagina with water that had been conveniently left in a basin and she indicated that I should undress and wash my penis. This was embarrassing. I had never undressed in front of a woman before. Maybe she would think my bum is too big or my calves too small.

She lay on the bed and I climbed on top of her. I had no idea of the mechanics of sex. I somehow thought my penis would mysteriously glide into her and so I was quite taken aback when seeing that I was clueless, she got a hold of it and thrust it inside her. As I moved in and out, still very embarrassed, I was thinking is this all there is to it? What's all the fuss about? And then, ah yes. This is nice. Yes, yes, very, very nice. And then oops! And suddenly it was all over. Thoughts of disappointment and disgust overwhelmed me.

I crept out of the dingy hotel with my head down and made my way back home, where I proceeded to spend the rest of the evening washing my penis, trying to erase my guilt. No, not an ideal introduction to sex.

THREE

UNIVERSITY AND ARGENTINA

Soon after the family holiday in Portugal, I left home and started my studies at Edinburgh University. I had just turned 17 but I had been anxious to leave home as my three elder brothers had all gone off to study in different parts of the country. I had worked hard and gotten excellent grades in my exams, enabling me to gain acceptance to university at a young age. I was in a hurry to show the world what I could do.

Edinburgh University was an august institution. Founded in the 17th century, it was the home of many illustrious philosophers, such as David Hume and the economist Adam Smith. In those days, only one in twenty gained entrance to university and we were treated as young gentlemen. Old men, decorated with medals from the Second World War, opened doors for us and called us "Sir." The tutors referred to us as "Mister" and were very respectful. It couldn't have been more different from the little town of Kirkcudbright where I grew up. There were students from all over the world and I never heard of any of the prejudices that I had grown up with, against the English, the Catholics or homosexuals. For a young man it was a wonderful city to explore; parks, gardens, museums, endless pubs of all shapes and sizes and some of the best golf courses in the world.

I was determined to have a glittering academic career, to outshine my brothers and to make a name for myself. The only problem was that I didn't particularly care for my subject, economics. It was more mathematical than I had anticipated and I found it hard going. However in those days it was not done to change your subject or to start over again. I was in a race to the top of the pile. I worked hard and I got good grades. To relieve the stress of studies I drank a lot of alcohol, especially on Friday nights. Saturdays were spent nursing a hangover until I was able to crawl out of bed and get ready for another evening of carousing. Drunkenness was seen as a badge of honour in those days, something to laugh about. The men had a separate social club from the women, the Men's Union and we would drunkenly sing songs about seduction and sex, always derogatory to women. Seemingly this had gone on for centuries and nobody was prepared to break the mould. I was a natural clown and in my drunken state I would get over my shyness. I would climb on a chair and do an impression of Al Jolson, who for the benefit of younger readers was a famous singer in the 1930's. He painted his face black, which would now consider politically incorrect, and yet he sung his hit song "I'm Just Wild About Harry" which seemed to me to be quite libertine.

Once suitably drunk, we would stagger up to the dance hall. Women were allowed to come to dance in the Men's Union on the weekends. They would line up along the sides of the room and we would cross the room and ask them to dance. Reason and sensitivity went out the window. All we were concerned with in our drunken states was sex. It rarely happened but was celebrated when it did. I remember later in life feeling pangs of remorse and contacting some of these women to offer my apologies. They were always kind and forgiving and said that this was how things happened in those days.

During summer holidays I would go off travelling. It was 1965 and I'd been told that Swedish women were extremely liberated and practiced free love. So off I went. I took a flight to Denmark. The alcohol, which was important for me at that time, was prohibitively expensive. However I found that by taking the tour of the Carlsberg factory I could get free beer. Next day I would go on a similar tour at the Tuborg brewery and this kept me going for a little while. The highlight for me was the Tivoli gardens, a sort of forerunner of Disneyland but done in very good taste. I then hitchhiked to Stockholm in Sweden. It was a little bit disappointing. The girls were not much different from girls back home. The only difference was that in Sweden a lot of couples lived together without being married. Back home on the other hand, in the mid 60's, couples were usually not allowed to stay in hotels together unless they could show a marriage certificate.

The following summer I decided to go to Israel. I took the train from London to Rome from where I was to fly to Israel. Unfortunately I couldn't find my train ticket. I had very little money, so there was no question of buying another ticket. Every time the ticket inspectors came, and they came frequently, I hid in the toilet. I couldn't lock the door otherwise a light would go on and show my presence inside. It was a long, long journey. Amazing how much you sweat when you are terrified. What if they throw me off the train? What if I miss my connection to Israel? The night was endless and eventually I fell asleep to be rudely awakened by Gestapo type guards, demanding to see my ticket. I made up a story at getting off at the next stop and paid a small fine. Finally the train arrived in Rome and I remember literally dancing on the platform, dishevelled and a little bit smelly but in love with the joys of life.

I spent a couple of months in Israel, working as an exchange student in an insurance company in Tel Aviv. The pace of life was fast. People seemed aggressive and it always seemed to me that they were having arguments when in fact they were just having friendly discussions. They were very hospitable, always happy to offer their guests food and drink. Israel at the time was the darling of the world. This was still a time of great idealism and the Kibbutz movement continued to flourish. It was before the Six Day War of 1967 and the annexation of the West Bank, and Israel was still seen as the underdog, surrounded by aggressive neighbours.

The World Cup football final between England and Germany was played during my stay. All the Israelis without exception fanatically supported the English because of the dark cloud of the Holocaust. They had conveniently forgotten that the British had turned away thousands of Jews fleeing from Europe after the Second World War to settle in what was then Palestine. I travelled all over Israel, visiting the Dead Sea, Masada and Eilat, then a completely deserted outpost on the border of Israel and Egypt.

It had been a great holiday but I was never tempted to go and live there. On my way home from Israel, I had another adventure on the train going from Rome to London. I was in a cabin with a group of students and we were having a wonderful time, singing songs and drinking wine. At one point in the south of France we ran out of wine and I got off at a train station to buy more. When I got back, to my horror, the train had gone with my luggage inside. I was distraught. The station master explained to me that there was an express train arriving shortly which would take me to Paris and if I took a taxi, with a bit of luck I might catch up with my original train which would take much longer to arrive in Paris. And so I did. When I arrived back in the cabin, everyone asked, "Where the hell have you been?" Of course nobody believed me when I told them my story.

Back home Edinburgh seemed cold and grey but it was great to see my girlfriend Sarah again. Condoms were not easily procured in those days. You had to hope that your barber might politely ask, "Anything for the weekend, Sir?" or else face a grim faced assistant in a chemist's shop; easier not to bother. How I wish that I had. Sarah got pregnant. This was a time when abortion was strictly illegal. I borrowed a large sum of money from my oldest brother Edward, and Sarah and I hitchhiked down to London for an illegal operation in a top class clinic. The operation went well and we hitchhiked back to Edinburgh feeling mightily relieved. I spent the summer holiday working in a dog meat factory to repay Edward. Sometimes I would be so smelly that I wouldn't be allowed on the bus coming home. I told my parents that I was on holiday in Greece and got my friend who was going there to send postcards for me. The only problem was the suntan. You don't easily get a suntan in Scotland, not even in the summer. And so I borrowed a sunlamp and made sure I was the right colour when I came home.

Most people would have been sufficiently traumatized by this experience to make sure it didn't happen again. I however operated strictly on the principle *Cock Rules, No Holds Barred*. And sure enough, a few months later Sarah was pregnant again; another trip to London, this time a rather cheaper operation. I lost touch with Sarah after leaving University. Bless you wherever you are. I often think of you.

More economic hardship as I struggled to make ends meet. My father of course knew nothing of this. I had to send him a weekly account of my expenses and I had to be unusually creative around this time, especially as we were not supposed to drink alcohol. I would write for example, *Late for lecture, had to take a taxi... 5 Shillings*. I'd inherited that one from one of my brothers and I knew my dad fell for it every time. It showed him how important our lectures were to us. He would always say, "Work hard and play hard, darling." Golf was important to him and so the accounts would continue. *Golf Balls... 10 Shillings*. "How many golf balls does he need?" he would ask my mother in wonderment. *Green Fees...12 Shillings*. Remember in those days 10 Shillings would buy 6 pints of beer, enough for a whole night.

One of the peculiarities of life in Scotland at this time was that the pubs would close at 10 p.m. Drinking up time was 10 minutes and then frequently the lights would go out and the doors would open, letting in the freezing cold. The barman would holler, "If yer no drunk by 10 o'clock, ye havn'a been tryin'. Away hame wi yese now!"

My studies were not going well. I had assumed that my grades would be sufficient for an academic career in a top university. It wasn't a bad result but it was not the result I'd been hoping for. I remember a cloud of depression hanging over my head for several days. I applied for about 20 different jobs but wasn't really interested in any of them and not surprisingly none of them were very interested in me. What I did do however, was make a huge amount of money.

Graduates in Economics were in short supply at the time and companies based in London were willing to pay them to fly down from Edinburgh and also to pay for their hotel. I arranged to have my interviews on consecutive days and thus avoid paying air fares each time. Multiply this by 20 and you can amass a huge pile of money. I am horrified by my dishonesty as I write but at the time it was all a bit of a game; a good story to tell my mates.

I eventually amassed enough money to join four school friends on a road trip to former Yugoslavia. This was the full blooming of youth in the playgrounds of Europe. One of the highlights of my trip was a five a side football match in Dubrovnik against a team of Russians.

This was 1968 and Russia had just invaded a rebellious Czechoslovakia and they were universally unpopular. These young Russians were staying in our campsite and were on an official goodwill mission. They challenged us to five a side football match.

Unbeknown to us they had publicised the match and when we turned up for what we thought was going to be a friendly kick about we were greeted by about 1,500 spectators cheering us on. Three of our team were good footballers and I was a reasonable goal keeper. However, the Russians were even better and at halftime we were losing 1-0. One of our team, Bruce, who wasn't much of a footballer, claimed injury and the Russians agreed to let us use a local person as a substitute. It turned out that he was a professional footballer of some renown and we managed to beat the Russians 2-1. It was as if we had won the war single handed and John, our goal scorer was carried off the pitch above the heads of an adoring crowd. The Russians were gracious in defeat and presented us with winner's medals; a happy end to a great day.

At the end of that summer I reluctantly returned to Scotland. I had unsuccessfully applied to do a course at the Harvard Business School and my best offer was to do a Masters Degree at Strathclyde University in Glasgow in Marketing. I decided to accept the offer even though since the age of thirteen, I had had strong reservations about advertising and marketing in general and the lies they told. Strathclyde was one of the new redbrick universities and a huge anticlimax after Edinburgh University. There was no university campus as such and students tended to live at home with their parents. There was nobody to open doors and call you "Sir." Glasgow itself in the 1960's was grey and dingy. There were often fights on the streets when the pubs closed, especially on a Saturday night. If Rangers (the Protestant football team) were playing Celtic (the Catholic team) that day, it was usually mayhem.

The course material seemed light and unsubstantial after the rigorous standards of Edinburgh University and I drifted along without doing a lot of work. One blessing was that I had a car by this time which gave me more confidence in myself, especially in my dealings with women.

A thesis was an important part of the Masters Degree in Marketing. I knew a lot about the poultry industry, having worked at my father's poultry factory in the summer holidays. The central part of the thesis involved interviewing 350 Glasgow householders about their egg preferences. At least that is what I told my supervisor. In fact I interviewed my mother and read a little around the subject and made up the rest. It must have been good enough because my supervisor swallowed it. I remember seeing my results being quoted years later in some learned journal. Again, I had no remorse at the time. It was a good story to entertain my mates with, in my role as a sort of offbeat clown.

Glasgow was particularly damp that winter and I was desperate to find a job overseas, somewhere sunny. I was delighted to get an offer from the Bank of London and South America, to be based in Argentina. I was to be paid what was for me a huge salary and I readily took up the offer. The job started with a four month training course in London along with 15 other graduate trainees. I was one of the few trainees not to have come from Oxford or Cambridge and I must have been chosen on the strength of my Masters Degree, the fact that I was a very good golfer and that I claimed to speak French (not very well in truth), German (I hardly spoke any) and Arabic (I had only learned how to swear from my dad).

We learned Spanish and banking theory although I struggled with the latter and spent most of my leisure time partying and socialising with my cousins, I did well enough however to stay in the job. In early January I arrived in Rio de Janeiro to spend a week on my own to be joined later by other bank trainees. We would then move on to Buenos Aires in Argentina to start work. Unfortunately in all the excitement of leaving home, I had forgotten to bring much money with me. Nobody in those days in South America spoke English. I was very much out of my comfort zone and found suddenly that I had lost all confidence in myself. I had almost no money to buy food and I withdrew into my own little shell. I remember contacting a cousin of a cousin's cousin and being taken out to dinner at the Hilton Hotel. I waited till after the meal when my host had made his exit and grabbed the tip that he had left, enough to buy food for the next day!

Eventually the other trainees came. I borrowed some money and a few days later we arrived in Buenos Aires, a steaming hot city which was in the middle of their summer. The bank itself was a new building, a wonder of modern architecture and outside gathered many locals, eating snacks just outside the main door, taking advantage of the new phenomenon of air conditioning. I lived in a very nice apartment with two other trainees, Steve and Martin, and we spent a lot of time carousing with other expatriates and bank workers. I played golf at the Hurlingham Club for expats, where I remember they used to ring a bell at 5 pm to announce that tea was being served and that Queen Victoria was alive and well!

A few weeks after I arrived I was joined by my girlfriend Sandra who stayed in our flat and cooked for us. She was a lovely woman, intelligent and resourceful and she was able to enjoy the crazy clown side of my character. I remember one of the stupidest things I have ever done in my life. Our apartment was on the fifth floor of a block of apartments in central Buenos Aires and during one drunken night I seemed to find it amusing to fill up contraceptives with water and bomb the passersby in the street. I cringe as I write this, at the discomfort caused to innocent pedestrians, not to mention the danger. You'd be surprised how large and heavy a contraceptive filled with water can be. Eventually the porter came up in a rage. *"Eso es un quilombo!* This is a whorehouse!" he said. My workmates were highly amused the next day when I told the story and asked them the meaning of *quilombo.* I have come to believe that we all have some protective force, perhaps a guardian angel to help us round sticky corners and I am eternally grateful that nobody was hurt by my stupidity.

The work at the bank was incredibly mundane and boring. Management believed that we trainees should start at the bottom and in those days before the digital revolution, all calculations were done with a mechanical adding machine. I didn't readily volunteer my services at work and I was often left to my own devices, either writing letters home or occasionally sloping off to play golf. Golf was an important lifeline for me and as my father had predicted a passport to the upper echelons of Buenos Aires society.

I played with the big chief, the manager of our vast bank in Buenos Aires, and with wealthy businessmen and dignitaries of the San Andres Golf Club that I had joined. I remember being invited to a dinner reception with a number of ambassadors representing various countries from all over the world. I arrived with Sandra (a little bit late) and after dinner, one by one they got up and made flowery, self important speeches about international co-operation bla bla bla and words that didn't mean a great deal. Nobody expected me to speak at this august gathering but by now, well oiled with the finest of Argentinean wine, I got up and started to out flower everybody with the floweriest of flowery speeches, celebrating the birth of a great friendship between my native Scotland and Argentina. I embellished on the theme of how this great friendship would change the very world we lived in and more and more in this vein. I don't remember much else, except that I got a huge and sincere ovation for what had been for me a joke, a bit of a prank. I had found my role as a speech maker. My only task now was to be able to do it sober.

After six months in the bustling metropolis of Buenos Aires, fellow trainee Steve, Sandra and I moved to Mendoza, an idyllic town in the foothills of the Andes, in the centre of a thriving wine producing area. This was a more conservative area and on the advice of our local bank manager, we had to pretend that Sandra was my sister who had come for a holiday. She was older than I and was eager to be married but I was still very immature and not yet ready to make such a step. Much to the relief of my family she went back to the UK. She was such a resourceful person that she ended up having a successful business and a wonderful marriage.

Soon after Sandra left I went with the bank, as part of their table tennis team to play our Chilean counterparts in Vina del Mar. We would play table tennis during the day and in the evening the whole team would visit the brothel. I was the youngest person in the team and the only one unmarried. The brothel was quite a sociable place and we drank *pisco sour*, the local brew and chatted with the girls. I remember on the third night being in bed with a particularly beautiful girl and having the strong sensation of being with a body and not a person; so much energy and attention being devoted to chasing after girls, but for what? Something was wrong.

The trip was also remarkable because I bought a big bag of top quality marijuana. I remember being questioned by custom officials high in the Andes on the Argentinean border in the freezing cold and the marijuana slipping from under my shirt where it was hidden, down to my underpants. Luckily I didn't get searched because had it been discovered, the consequences in those days would have been extremely serious.

For the next six months of my stay in Mendoza until my eventual departure I got high almost every single night. I would stagger out of bed early in the morning to go to work in the bank. The work was still excruciatingly boring, adding up figures on the adding machine and looking on at an incredibly antiquated and inefficient banking system. I was powerless to do anything about it, had I even shown the slightest bit of interest in doing so.

Nights were for fun, girlfriends and parties. My flatmate Steve and I got on well and he was patient with my erratic and often drug induced behaviour. Just as a footnote, I found out 40 years later that Steve who was handsome, hard working and likeable, eventually became the CEO of the third largest bank in the world.

I entered completely into my role as clown and entertainer. I remember one evening when I was locked out of our first floor apartment which was directly above a cafe. I piled table upon table making a sort of stairway and managed to climb up to a balcony to the thunderous applause of the crowd below, a wonderful opportunity for me to make a speech.

Socializing after table tennis tournament in Chile

When I was high I wanted to lift everyone's spirit. I had a partner in crime, a local boy named Daniel and we were arrested for going the wrong way down a one way street. I made some stupid joke about only going one way and fortunately with all our fooling around the gun carrying police were helpless with laughter and sent us on our way. It was a charmed existence. We lived off the fat of the land. We finished work at 2 pm and usually spent the afternoon at the golf club. We made friends with an American, Colonel Ed Wolfe whom we nicknamed Lobo (Spanish for wolf). He was a hardnosed but very funny, charismatic man and we would often play golf together. He was in charge of a large contingent of the US Air

Force but refused to ever talk about what he and his men were doing there. At the time I was more interested in his friendship than questioning his motives for being there. Many years later I found out that the American Air Force was used to reinforce the power of the dictatorship of the day.

My career came to an abrupt end one evening when one of the bank's clients announced that he wanted to take me to a brothel to have sex with four bisexual women. We were to watch them have sex before joining in the fun but first I must take a pill, probably some sort of forerunner of Viagra. I remember being in a state of madness that whole evening as we watched the two female couple having sex together. One bizarre memory that lingers is of my colleague having sex while puffing away at an enormous cigar in his mouth.

The next morning I was unable to get out of bed and the manager of the bank by this time was growing short of patience with my behaviour. He sent a doctor to confirm that I was genuinely ill and unfortunately our cleaning lady who happened to be there that day, let the doctor in. He came into my room and with his finger he prised open one eye and announced me to be *endrogado*, i.e. doped up to the eyeballs. This did not go down well with the powers that be and they recommended that I be sacked. This was all very convenient because I had had enough of the bank and I knew that back home in Scotland my father was in the process of dying.

Some days later just before leaving Mendoza, the bank held a reception to celebrate some anniversary or other. This was a perfect opportunity to make a farewell speech. I talked about how the bank manager had begged me on bended knees to stay but that unfortunately destiny was taking me elsewhere and that I was so sorry to leave everybody. It was very dramatic and they all loved it. The manager was cringing and looking irate. He had sacked me after all but by the end of the evening even he could see the funny side of the situation. The head office of the bank in Buenos Aires offered to send me to another branch in the south but by now I had had enough and knew I had to go home to visit my ailing father in Scotland.

FOUR

Yoga and Formentera

My father was unconscious when I arrived home from Argentina and he died later that evening. He had been kept alive until me and my brother Donald (who had been working in South Africa) arrived home together

I felt sad about his death. He had done so much for me. Yet as the months rolled by, I also felt a sense of relief that there was no longer a powerful authority figure attempting to dictate the course of my life. I felt however that I should stay in the UK to be in close proximity to my mother, now a widow. I got a very well paid job, working in the research department of a firm of management consultants in central London. The job was certainly more fulfilling than working in the bank but I was pretty lost and miserable. I drank quite a lot of alcohol, smoked dope and dedicated a lot of my energies to playing golf and seducing women, with varying degrees of success.

To compound my misery I contracted a type of venereal disease which refused to go away, nonspecific urethritis. The treatment involved abstaining from alcohol, so being a logical sort of person I upped my consumption of marijuana. I made frequent visits to the venereal disease clinic in the basement of Paddington Hospital. It was considered a huge disgrace at the time and I remember well being greeted in the men's section of the clinic by a degenerate type of man who would say with a mocking cackle, "I know what you've been up to, you dirty bugger. Now go and pee in the glass."

It was after one of these visits that I was coming home on the London Underground. There was a little shop selling magazines and for some unknown reason I spontaneously picked up a magazine about yoga. There was an article that really caught my attention which said something to the effect, "Do this exercise and then do that one every day and you will be happy."

I was excited and immediately interested. Could it be so easy? I had always been good at applying myself, passing exams and getting good grades; obviously worth a try. Very little was known about yoga in those days. There were few books about it and very few yoga classes. However I purchased a book by Richard Hittleman and started to practice yoga every day much to the amusement of my brothers and cousins. I had always played the role of clown and so reluctantly I played along with them. In my heart though I knew I'd found something of importance. Some weeks later after finishing my work I went to my first yoga class. It was in the Sivananda Yoga

Centre in Earls Court. I entered the yoga studio. The class was about to start. The room was lit by candles, incense was burning and Sanskrit chants were playing in the background. I found a mat and sat down. The teacher was a young monk with long hair and a flowing, orange robe.

"Any particular reason why you are wearing your shoes?" he asked me.

"Gosh no, sorry," I muttered. I took them off. I hadn't realised that yoga was traditionally done barefoot. And then the class started.

We were taught how to breathe. Almost immediately my mind slowed down. We were guided through the Salute to the Sun series of exercises. Words such as reverence and humility seem to take on a new meaning for me. The pace was very slow. We held postures for a long time. The longer we held the postures the easier they became. The mind became more and more peaceful. And then we moved onto chanting sacred Sanskrit words. Friends, I was transported to another realm.

By the time we had finished with several minutes of deep relaxation lying on the floor, I was like a new man. We were invited to drink herbal tea, another first for me, and I got a chance to ask our teacher a host of questions. "Is it really possible to survive without eating meat?" I asked incredulously. He assured me that it was and that he, a picture of perfect health, hadn't eaten meat or fish for many years. I continued to come to his classes and practice assiduously every day at home and even in the lunch break at work. One day I was in the store room in the basement of our company, standing on my head when the boss came in.

"Great Christ!" he said. I thought I was in for a bollocking and might even lose my job, but he said, "No no, continue! I remember seeing people doing this when I worked out East. If it helps to distress you then do continue, old boy. God, if I were younger I'd probably take it up myself."

I talked with one or two people about becoming a vegetarian. Remember, it was pretty unknown in those days. There were very few vegetarian restaurants in London. You'd mention it and people would conjure up images of fakirs lying on beds of nails or emaciated ascetics with runny noses. I decided to try it and see how I felt. My plan was to just eat meat on weekends when I would go and visit my uncle and cousins. However, come the weekend I found I had no desire to eat meat whatsoever. Nothing could have been easier for me than giving up meat and fish and I loved my new regime.

My yoga classes were going well and I was becoming more and more intrigued by Transcendental Meditation as taught by Maharishi Mahesh Yogi, the famous mentor of the Beatles. I signed up to do the meditation course and a few days later turned up at my teacher's house, very self consciously bringing incense, candles and a bunch of flowers. My teacher seemed okay, quite serious and intense but not unlikeable.

I asked him, "Look, if I do this twice a day as I'm supposed to, how long will it take till I'm enlightened?"

He hummed and hawed for a while and finally said in measured tones, "Difficult to give a precise time, but I'd say around 6 years."

"Six years," I replied, "that's a long time," thinking to myself, Christ, I'll be thirty by then! Well, if that's what it takes to find eternal bliss, I reasoned, then what the heck, I might as well go for it. And so I handed over the money and he lit the candles and the incense for the initiation ceremony to begin.

I was a bit nervous and when my teacher whispered in my ear the secret mantra that I was to repeat for 20 minutes, I had to ask him to repeat it. I would start to meditate and then a few seconds later I would forget it. This happened several times and each time he would repeat it more and more urgently. Suddenly I collapsed into hysterical laughter and this went on for several minutes. My teacher didn't seem terribly amused.

Apparently this had never happened before. Eventually I managed to calm myself down and 20 minutes later I said my goodbyes, feeling calm and relaxed. Okay, I thought, this is going to take a lot longer than I had imagined, but hell, I've paid my money and I'm going to go for it.

It was becoming clearer and clearer to me that I couldn't stay in a regular nine to five job. I wanted travel and adventure and the company of other seekers. I gave up my job, much to the consternation of my nearest and dearest and signed up for a holiday package in Mallorca, an island on the coast of Spain. I was thinking it would be nice to have a holiday that would enable me to be in the sun, practice yoga and meditation and at the same time enjoy a wonderful social life. The holiday was organised fun in a resort for young people based around sex, sun and alcohol. Evenings they had events such as bingo, darts, beer drinking and knobbly knee competitions and more of this genre. I felt like some sort of alien and was completely miserable. I decided to cut short my holiday and take the twelve hour boat trip to the island of Formentera next to Ibiza where I had school friends staying.

Ah, Formentera! A magnet for yogis, mystics and hippies from all over the world; *una isla escandalisada,* an island of ill repute, as a Spanish newspaper called it. The article was adorned with pictures of naked hippies on a beach, all bums and tits being discretely erased. This was still the time of Franco and his ferocious police force Guardia Civil. But that didn't stop the fun. There was a guy called Alex, teaching yoga and massage and I really looked up to him. I was practicing yoga every day, doing my Transcendental Meditation and although I drank a little alcohol, I had given up marijuana. I was eager for a teacher and Alex seemed to fit the role. I studied massage and this being the sort of place where there were no holds barred, all was done as a group, completely naked. Easier said than done. I never managed more than 10 minutes without getting an erection, but then my meditation technique would kick in. Breathe! Repeat the mantra! I would say to myself and gradually I would calm down. Indeed, this became something to show off whenever I was lucky enough to find a woman willing to witness the spectacle. I would get excited then get a great erection and then I'd shut my eyes and down it went in a matter of seconds.

After a few weeks I became disillusioned with my mentor Alex. One friend confided that when he was giving her a massage he started to lick her vagina. I felt disappointed with him and I started to look for another teacher. One day I was strolling along the beach, when I ran into a very interesting middle aged man. He was a tall, imposing figure, a German baron by the name of Ronimund Von Bissing. As a boy he had had a lot of contact through his aristocratic parents with the Russian mystic Gurdjieff and was now a follower of an Indonesian shaman and healer called Bapak. Bapak became something of a phenomenon in the 1950's, especially amongst the followers of Gurdjieff. The practice he taught was called Subud. The idea was to simply surrender to an unseen power and let whatever happened happen. Bapak would give this energy or "open" a follower who would then open others so that they in turn could surrender to this unseen power. Ronimund had been given this power by Bapak and I was anxious to experience it. I arranged to come to one of the weekly meetings which was scheduled for Saturday night.

Saturday night though, I ran into some friends in the local bar and by the time I remembered my date with Ronimund, I was drunk. Undeterred I cycled off to his home. The men did their ceremony separately from the women who were led by Ronimund's wife Sofia. This was a bit of a disappointment but I quickly reminded myself in my drunken state that I was here for enlightenment, not for sex.

The service, called *latihan*, lasted about thirty minutes. Ronimund laid his hands upon me to transmit the power and open me. People around me started to make all sorts of noises. There were chickens and donkeys, opera singers and everything in between as they surrendered to this unseen power. I felt absolutely nothing, only a modicum of shame for turning up drunk. The following day I made my way to Ronimund's large mansion and confessed to him about having been drunk the previous evening. I asked if he might open me again. I think he liked the fact that I'd been honest enough to confess and he told me to come the following week.

The same men were there as last week. This time I was stone cold sober and after receiving the energy from Ronimund, I settled into the process. Undisturbed by all the weird noises around me, I kept saying half aloud, half to myself, I surrender, I surrender, I let go. And low and behold, I had the most glorious experience of awakening. I felt ecstatically happy. I looked up at the stars, twinkling through the large bay windows and I felt peace. I came to realise that I carried around with me some sort of subconscious fear and in these precious moments I felt utter love and peace.

I hurried off to the bar, anxious to tell all my friends about my newfound peace. Bad move. Nobody was very interested and one guy started to malign Ronimund calling him a "bread freak" which meant a materialistic person in the hippie lingo of the day.

Although this experience was never quite repeated in subsequent *latihan* sessions, it was yet another reminder that we are much more than meets the eye.

It was a time of friendship and experimentation. I smoked marijuana again, had a memorable LSD trip and took the local drug called Dormodina which was supposed to be a sleeping pill. Except that it was nothing of the sort. It simply made you lose your balance and made you as horny as hell. One summer evening there were about 12 of us sitting in a circle at a party and we'd all taken a tab of Dormodina. Showing what I thought was great initiative I took off all my clothes and announced that I was ready for sex. Everyone looked at me, nobody came forward. A few of the men snickered to themselves and I started to feel incredibly foolish. Fortunately one brave young German *fraulein* undressed and lay down in front of me. Thank you, dear *fraulein* for your kindness. You saved the day for me.

Eventually though, it was time to move on. I had been so happy on the island and I wanted to stay forever but none of the projects that I'd been considering came to fruition and very reluctantly I was compelled to leave, a very different person from the one who had arrived a few months earlier.

FIVE

CALIFORNIA

In January 1973, I arrived in California. I wanted to be part of the blossoming awakening of consciousness that was happening there. People were going back to the land and building communities. Yogis were coming from India and attracting many followers. The people I met were very hospitable and there was a tremendous sense of cooperation. I hitchhiked everywhere and often the driver would invite me to stay overnight. There were "crash pads" peoples' private homes where travellers could come and stay overnight free of charge.

I had read about a community north of Sacramento which followed the teachings of the Russian mystic Gurdjieff and I made my way there. A very kind driver helped me look for the community. It was near Grass Valley and we spent an hour or so searching for it but it was nowhere to be found. It was getting late and he suggested that I might like to stay in the community where he was living. It turned out that it was a group of people who followed the teachings of an Indian guru, Paramahansa Yogananda, who had come from India in the 1920's and who had been instrumental in introducing yoga to America. He died in 1952 but one of his chief disciples, an American, Swami Kriyananda, had set up a spiritual community in his honour.

The residents lived in geodesic domes and sang devotional chants, written by Yogananda twice daily, always accompanied by a harmonium. I loved these songs and I loved the people living there even though it all seemed very, very strange and unfamiliar. I read Yoganada's epic book "Autobiography of a Yogi" and I felt deeply inspired by his imagery and his yogic philosophy. He describes his spiritual experiences, memories of past lives and meeting his guru. The book cast its spell over me in the same way it has done with millions of other seekers. I found myself looking around every corner, hoping to see visions of saints and sages.

The only trouble with Grass Valley in winter is the rain; torrential rain every single day. I'd come from the UK to get away from the rain and rather reluctantly I left the community and headed south. I ended up in Santa Barbara, in a community called The Brotherhood of the Sun. It was headed by Norm Paulsen, a charismatic leader who had also been a disciple of Yogananda. I was attracted to this community because it was based in the country and I imagined that we would be following the yoga precepts of Yogananda; nothing of the sort. Although Norm espoused universal principles of love and peace, his approach bordered on Christian fundamentalism. What was worse for me was that divergent views were not tolerated.

The organisation ran several farms and I ended up in a community of about 20 young people on an apple orchard just east of Ojai. It was winter and it was freezing cold at night. We met twice daily for long meditations and spent the day working hard. I didn't fit in. Nobody seemed to have a concept of the universality of religion. You were either with Norm and part of the sect or you were a rebel. They promised peace and enlightenment if we could just stay and toe the line. I was on a mission. I wanted peace and enlightenment and although it seemed like torture, I stayed on. I reasoned that a few months or even years of hard discipline was a small price to pay for eventual bliss. I allowed myself one symbol of rebellion. I decided to eat only raw foods, mainly fruit. This did not go down well. I was branded "a food tripper". Norm did at the beginning try to reason with me and help me. On one occasion, seeing me tired and a bit poorly (probably due to my extreme diet) he took me in his arms and squeezed me hard. As I left his embrace I felt rejuvenated, a totally new person. He was a great healer and a wonderful orator. People were spellbound in his presence which is why so many people were able to believe every word he said.

The months passed and I became even more miserable. Norm had spies, listening to my conversations and making notes of the books I was reading, which were mainly about yoga and mysticism. The only saving grace was that spring had arrived and the weather was no longer ferociously cold. I decided that it was time to leave but my passport which needed to be renewed had not yet arrived from the British Embassy. Things came to a head during one of Norm's periodic visits.

"How ya doin', brother?" he asked. He was a huge man and he towered over me.

"Well, not so good, Norm," and I started to recount some of the things that were troubling me.

He leaned over menacingly. "I want you outa here by sundown."

Ok, I said. "I hope we are still friends."

"Depends what ya mean by friends. Get outa here and don't talk to anyone before ya go."

I thought he might hit me and so I beat a hasty retreat. I was quite happy to go but my only worry was that my passport hadn't arrived and I didn't like the idea of leaving without it. Fortunately, a few minutes later, Norm's chief henchman handed me my passport which he claimed had just arrived that morning. I left the community at sundown and continued with my wanderings.

It was getting warmer and so I decided to head north on the famous Highway 101 to visit my cousin in San Francisco. On the way there I got picked up by a woman driving a truck. She pricked up her ears when I told her the story of my life and she invited me to come and stay in her little community in Big Sur. The community was headed by a guy called Bret. He had a long beard, psychedelic clothes and two wives. Bret was convinced that the stresses of modern life made it necessary to take LSD as a medicine on a weekly basis to avoid the energy pollution caused by negative thought forms.

They lived in an idyllic house with stunning views, overlooking the ocean, hardly a stressful environment! They were very hospitable and their almost totally fruitarian diet suited the strict regime that I was following. I arrived 2 days before the weekly LSD trip and I was toying with the idea of taking up their invitation to join them. They insisted that their LSD was very pure, straight from the lab and when the big day arrived, bright and sunny I decided to give it a go. The tab was tiny, barely visible to the naked eye and looked innocuous. I swallowed it and spent the next 15 minutes looking at the moon still in the morning sky. It looked so feminine and inviting. I was wondering why nothing dramatic was happening. My hand drifted down to my penis. The moment I touched it, I had an orgasm; a big one! Then it dawned on me, yes, I was tripping! I started to feel that I had woken up for the first time in my life. That I had spent the last quarter century in a deep sleep. And yet, so many people had told me that LSD was dangerous and that the visions were false and simply drug-induced. I instantly knew that this was laughable and that my present version of reality was the most valid one I had ever experienced. I took off all my clothes and wandered about naked in the sunshine. I seemed to understand the interconnection of time and space.

I went back to my hosts who were all tripping in the main house.

"Wake up, wake up!" I cried joyfully. They laughed. They'd heard it all before.

"Go and talk with the trees," advised Bret and so I did; enormous Douglas Firs. I had never seen such big ones. I put my arms round one and felt my connection with the Divine and so it went on; insight after insight. Late in the day I was still tripping and starting to become exhausted. Bret gave me vitamin C to bring me down. One of the wives asked me if I would have swapped the experience for a million dollars. What a strange question I thought.

"No way," I replied! "Money could never buy such insight and bliss."

The next day was hard. It was worse than a hangover. I felt as if the energy surrounding my body had been punctured and I felt incredibly vulnerable. However, I gradually recovered and soon I was like a man transformed. Looking back, I realize it was one of the most important experiences of my life. Never again would I doubt the interconnection of all beings and that our mission in life is to wake up and re-discover our divine essence. I went up to the Bay area for a few days as planned and then made the decision to hitchhike down to South America. I had heard of a fruitarian community there. It was rumoured to be in Ecuador and I was determined to find it.

I had a strange experience just before the Mexican border. I decided to call in at an ashram, run by followers of Paramahansa Yogananda in Encinitas, just south of Los Angeles. Just before arriving, the young people I was getting a ride with offered me a joint. I hadn't realised it but it was a sort of reinforced hash, extra strong, called skunk. I arrived at the gate of the ashram completely stoned and was about to ring the bell, when a car pulled up beside me. It was a beautiful blonde girl driving a large convertible.

"Wanna lift?" she asked.

"Sure," I replied without thinking and climbed in. I was travelling with a woman I had befriended the night before and out of respect for her, it didn't feel right to go off with this lovely, friendly driver. She dropped us off where we were headed. I often wondered about this chance encounter, about the timing and the fact that I wasn't looking for a lift. Surely things like that don't happen in real life. I had the strong feeling that Yogananda was protecting the ashram from someone unfit at that time to enter; all very strange.

The journey down to South America was long and arduous. At one point in Mexico, I had to take a bus but hitchhiking was normally very easy as there was virtually only one road, the Pan American Highway that went from the American border to Panama. Sometimes I would get a lift in the back of a lorry for hundreds of miles. One of the highlights of this journey was crossing the border from Mexico into neighbouring Guatemala just after dawn had broken. There were green cloud capped hills and smiling indigenous people in their colourful garments, one of the most beautiful sights I had ever seen. It is a memory that has stayed with me all my life. As I write these words by Lake Atitlan in Guatemala, I realise that it was this memory that helped spark off the spontaneous decision to come here that I had made several months ago.

Soon after, I got a lift from two beautiful English girls and the boyfriend of one of them. They invited me to come with them to Lake Atitlan. This time though, the lizard brain did not kick in. I was on a mission and I continued heading south until I eventually reached Panama.

From Panama I took a flight from Venezuela as the Pan American Highway made an abrupt stop at the thick jungle. All this travel, around 3,000 miles in about ten days, had taken its toll physically on me. I caught a high fever and felt very weak. As often happens, fate intervened to look after me. Desperate to get out of the capital city of Caracas, I took a bus to a neighbouring beauty spot. I met a young man on the bus who told me that his father was a pastor from the US and he might be able to help me. His dad did indeed lend me a caravan to stay in, free of charge. I had the good sense to know not to eat. I drank only water and let nature take its course. The pastor popped by from time to time but I could barely move. He gave me a book which was a commentary on the Lord's Prayer, "Our Father, etc…" which I recited ardently, hoping for a miracle cure. I did get better eventually but by now I'd had enough of travelling and was eager to get home. I managed to get a cheap flight to Luxembourg and from there, sleeping rough from time to time, I hitchhiked back to my family in Scotland.

Just as a couple of footnotes:

~ *A couple of years ago I did some research about Norm's community, The Brotherhood of the Sun. It turns out that they had been stockpiling guns in anticipation of Armageddon, when they envisaged hoards of hungry outsiders attempting to steal their crops. Norm, it transpired, towards the end of his life had periodic problems with prescription drugs. He died in 1991.*

~ *I found out that 20 years later, when I visited Ecuador on my honeymoon, that the fruitarian community did in fact exist in the south of Ecuador but that most of the residents had left because their teeth had started to fall out due to their overly strict fruitarian diet.*

SIX

INDIA AND AUSTALASIA

My mother was delighted to see me back home. She felt relieved that I hadn't joined a sect and that I seemed healthy enough. When I announced that I was now a fruitarian, she laughed and told me to go and graze in the garden. Soon enough though, I realised that this diet was far too extreme for my body and particularly unsuitable for the Scottish climate and so I resumed my normal vegetarian diet.

I wasn't sure where to go next. Remaining in the UK was out of the question. I wanted to go somewhere warm. My cousin Charlie had a successful business in Australia and he had offered me a job in his textile business. I knew it was not the sort of work I really wanted but it was comforting to know that if I headed there, I would be warmly received.

Later that summer I attended a Yoga and Mystics Conference in London and one of the principal speakers was Swami Gitananda who had an ashram in Pondicherry in the south of India. He was a charming and charismatic Indian American, a large barrel chested man and a former wrestler. He was an amazing communicator full of mind boggling stories and seemingly endless knowledge of all subjects. It wasn't in his nature to say "I don't know" and he was always able to improvise a convincing story, not always true, as I later found out. He also had certain yogic powers. He could slow his heartbeat to three or four beats per minute in front of medical observers. I told him about my first thirst for enlightenment and my desire to study yoga and he painted a glowing picture of his ashram. I was so taken by his charm and aura of strength that I signed up to do a three months Yoga Teacher Training Course starting in October.

You are probably wondering at this point how I managed to make enough money to sustain this travelling lifestyle. I had some savings from my last job which I eventually used up but mostly I lived very frugally. In the community in California for example, I worked for my keep. In addition, I was part of a family business, inherited from my father and technically I had the right to ask my family for money from time to time. They were often reluctant to support my wanderings but when it became necessary, my brother Donald whom I loved dearly and who had always supported me, would make sure that I had just enough money to get by. I knew that my oldest brother Edward, who had taken upon himself the role of head of the family, wanted me to settle down and get a proper job but for the moment I didn't face too much opposition from the family. I was lucky in that my mother had her three other sons, which was a comfort for her after the death of my father and I felt it was fine for me to pursue my travels.

I arrived in India in October 1973 with my friend Shirley who had also signed up to do the course. In Bombay we were greeted with a cacophony of noise in the streets, the likes of which I had never heard before. The smells and the colours! It was all quite overwhelming. We eventually made our way down to Pondicherry in the south east corner of India. Feeling grimy and travel weary we made our way straight to the beach. We undressed and went into the sea, Shirley in a bright red bikini. When we emerged a few minutes later there were upwards of a hundred men watching the spectacle. Hurriedly Shirley got dressed. Later that evening we went to a nightclub. No women, only men. They would beg my permission for just one dance with Shirley. Women didn't seem to have a strong presence in India in those days.

We had arrived in Pondicherry a few days before the course started because we wanted to visit the community of Auroville. The community was the vision of a French Egyptian woman, known simply as "The Mother." She was the wife of a French diplomat and after her divorce she stayed on in Pondicherry to join the ashram of the mystic and poet Sri Aurobindo. A large following grew around them and in 1968 her brainchild, the community of Auroville was founded, a few miles north of Pondicherry. Hundreds of young seekers from all over the world arrived to give shape to her vision. Their first task was to plant trees because the area had been desertified by the British 200 years earlier to build their ships. When I came to Auroville in 1973 the planting had just begun but when I came again in 2019 there were some 400 square miles of lush jungle and around 3,000 inhabitants in the community. The central temple called the Matrimandir had just been started when I first came but had been completed by the time I returned in 2019. It was a magnificent structure, a temple of the future which invoked in me memories of my LSD trip.

A few days later we arrived at the ashram of Swami Gitananda. Discipline was extremely strict. Late arrival at 6 a.m. morning yoga on more than one occasion meant expulsion from the ashram. For the first month the discipline was tolerable. I felt that I was learning precious yoga techniques that were secret and according to Swami unavailable elsewhere. He was a wonderfully entertaining speaker and we were all convinced that this was the only place to be if we were to be accomplished yogis. Almost all other yogic establishments and gurus were condemned by Swami.

Having paid for a three months I strongly felt that I had to stay the course.

Me in Peacock posture

I could hear the voice of my late father telling me that
you must work hard in order to achieve what you want, in
my case yogic bliss. Anyway, it was hell and I counted the
days until my release. Swami had a violent temper and
woe betide anyone who contradicted or challenged him.
And yet I look back on him with a great deal of respect.
He did a lot of charitable work in the community and was
in essence a good man and I did learn a lot about yoga.
As well as all the yogic postures, we learned advanced
breathing techniques, basic chiropractic manipulations
and numerology, the science of numbers. My favourite
part of the day was singing the Sanskrit mantras that
Swami taught us. Afterwards I learned that these yogic

techniques were indeed available elsewhere but I was happy nevertheless to have learned them. On certain rare occasions I was ecstatically happy as when for example we would cycle down to the beach for morning yoga and a swim in the sea.

The days dragged on but finally the departure date loomed. Just before leaving Gitananda gave me permission to visit the temple town of Tiruvannamalai which was in 1973 a little known pilgrimage centre. It had been the home of a famous saint, Ramana Maharshi who had left his body in 1952. He was in silence for the latter part of his life and taught his disciples using a chalkboard. His teachings were based on rigorous self enquiry, endlessly asking the question "Who am I?"

Dusk was falling when I arrived. Searching around for a place to stay I met an elderly lady, a devotee of Ramana who had been living there for many years. She invited me to stay with her. Her late husband Arthur Osborne had been the main chronicler of the life of Ramana and it was fascinating to be in her company. I walked around the sacred mountain Arunachala where Ramana had spent many years meditating in a cave. Although I had arrived with an extremely agitated mind, I felt almost immediately a wonderful calm and the presence of the Divine. Reluctantly I made my way back to Gitananda's ashram.

Finally, just before Christmas, the course finished. We got our hard earned yoga teaching certificates and we all went our separate ways. I was free at last and it was with great relief that I took a plane to Australia. I had a two day stop in Perth. My first images of this city will always stay in my mind. After the chaos of India, the noise, the dirt and the multitudes, Perth seemed so clean, quiet and ordered. Office workers wore shorts and long socks and looked well scrubbed. No bargaining with shopkeepers. Everything was well run and convenient.

My cousin Charlie in Sydney welcomed me with open arms, even though he was a little bit surprised with my hippie-like appearance. International travel was less well known in those days and I was the first of our massive extended family to visit him in Australia. I had changed my name to Rodger (my middle name) based on my numerology studies and it somehow seemed a more masculine name, more appropriate to my image of the rugged outdoor life of Australia.

Spending time with Charlie and his family was a great treat but I wasn't ready to settle in a huge city like Sydney and I decided to move on to New Zealand. It seemed like the end of the world. I couldn't go any further without heading back towards Europe. The people were warm and friendly and it felt like a good place for me to settle. I chose what was then a little surfing town called Mount

Maunganui in the Bay of Plenty. It was well named. I had never seen such a variety of fruit, many of them as yet unknown in Europe.

I rented a small house, almost without furniture (I was a yogi after all!) and set about advertising my yoga classes. I knew something about marketing and so I got the local paper to write about my extensive yogic training and plastered the town with handmade posters. Swami Gitananda had instilled in me a supreme confidence in my knowledge and my abilities and I really thought I had something precious to teach the world. I think we can often teach really well when we have discovered something new. It is our enthusiasm for the subject and our dedication which can inspire others. I think I was an inspiring teacher and I had a faithful following.

I remember the very first posture of my very first yoga class. It involved lying on your back, bending your legs and drawing your knees towards you with your arms. It was called the gas relief posture. And as I announced this to my students, I inadvertently let out some gas. My students thought I had done it on purpose and they laughed uproariously, always a good way to start a class. I loved New Zealand, there seemed to be a feeling of contentment. It was "God's own country" as they used to say.

As winter approached I started to feel the cold. It was becoming too much like Scotland and I started to get itchy feet. One of the joys of travelling is that as soon as you are slightly inconvenienced you can move on.

Just before leaving I attended an encounter group on a remote island north of Auckland, New Zealand's biggest city. Encounter groups were very much a thing of the 60's and 70's where we were encouraged to voice our feelings about ourselves and about other people in a "no holds barred," atmosphere. It was being run by Ed, an older American guy who looked like a wizard with his long hair, his pointed nose, his golden necklace and long black cloak.

It all seemed very threatening to me. In Scotland we had been brought up to hide our feelings. Stiff upper lip and be a man and all that sort of thing. At one point I had to stand up naked in front of the group and talk about my perceptions of my body and so I began, "My feet are too big, my calves are too small and my bum is too big," and more in this vein. I looked up. I hadn't noticed it before but they were all grinning and laughing. "Your body is fine," said Ed. Everyone agreed. "You need to get yourself a new self-image, brother," he continued. Little by little I felt able to express myself more. It was all very friendly. There were three men, including myself, and four women. We paired up. Myself and another guy slept with one woman each. Ed slept with the other two.

"Well, he's the leader after all," I reasoned to myself.

A couple of days after the Encounter Group I received a visit from some people who had heard about me via one of the articles I had had published about myself. They told me that they channelled very high beings from another galaxy and that I was an important member of their group and that I should go and live with them to help in their endeavours to welcome extraterrestrials. This was before UFO sightings had become well known and extraterrestrials were very much considered to be loony imaginings of lost people. I was slightly flattered and was longing to see a UFO and it seemed like a good idea to stay with them and find out more.

Grandmother did the channelling of the voices of extraterrestrials and her daughter and son-in-law looked after the house. The son-in-law worked with a bulldozer and spent his spare time building a landing circle for extraterrestrials. I was sceptical. Surely, if they'd come all the way from another galaxy they would know how to land. I was looking for concrete evidence of extraterrestrials but I saw none. Yes, it was flattering for a few days to be told how important I was but I started to realise that I was just part of someone's fantasy. I certainly had a long beard and Indian clothes and I looked like a wise man and sometimes I even talked like one but fairly quickly I realised that it was time to move on. I flew from New Zealand and ended up in the subtropical town of Brisbane in Queensland, Australia.

After a few months there, doing odd jobs and studying massage it started to become stiflingly hot as summer approached and so I headed south to Sydney where I had cousins. Back in those days British citizens were eligible for unemployment benefits and could even get an Australian passport after one year's residence there. With this money I enrolled in a college to study acupuncture and osteopathy. It seemed like a good idea to have a profession that I could practice anywhere in the world. Unfortunately my studies didn't go too well. I had studied so hard in the past and I wasn't sufficiently motivated to start learning a new subject. It takes a long time and a lot of effort to develop the sensitivity and knowledge to practice acupuncture and osteopathy and I was by nature impatient. The paradox is that I could often cure people with my osteopathic manipulations and with acupuncture. When you have just learned something new, you transmit to the patient your belief in the healing process. They were also intrigued by my beard and exotic clothes. I looked like a healer.

However the healing didn't work quite so well on myself. I remember going to a hospital for dental treatment. It was offered free of charge in hospitals as opposed to a normal dental clinic where it was quite expensive. I explained to the dentist that I was an acupuncturist and I would not need an anaesthetic. I had been taught the anaesthesia points a few days earlier, though I had never actually used them. Very excited the dentist called out all his medical colleagues to watch the operation. Oh my God! It hurt like hell. I must have gotten the wrong points. With so many fascinated spectators, I had to pretend there was no pain. I breathed very, very deeply as I tried to distance myself from the pain. It didn't help much though and I left the hospital somewhat bruised and battered.

I decided to open a massage clinic in Paddington, an up and coming area of Sydney. Again, I used all my marketing skills to get an article written about me and I waited for the customers to arrive. For some reason, all the clients seemed to think that it was a massage parlour for homosexuals. I suspect they had read between the lines of the newspaper article and they had got the wrong message. They went away disappointed and I was disappointed too. After a while I gave up. I didn't have the perseverance to get a healing practice off the ground.

Sydney was a delightful place to live. I have never been keen on big cities but Sydney in those days was quite special. The eastern part of the city where I lived was surrounded by beaches and there were far fewer cars on the road than nowadays. The women I was attracted to seemed to be so forthcoming. They always seemed willing to make the first move, to call you up and arrange a date. This was so refreshing. In Europe, I had often found it difficult making the first move in a relationship for fear of rejection and this was a welcome change. Despite the attractions of Australia, the openness of the culture, the natural environment and wonderful weather, after a couple of years I started to feel that it was time to move on. I longed for Europe with its variety of cultures, all within easy reach of each other and I was also beginning to miss family and friends.

A very eventful journey home via the Pacific Ocean followed. I stopped in Fiji, where I attended a prayer meeting led by A C Prabupatha, the founder of the Hare Krishna movement. We chanted the Hare Krishna mantra and it was a vibrant joyous atmosphere. At one point he looked up at me and asked me where I was from. I told him I was from Scotland at which point he said "Ah, Glasgow," nothing more, and then he let out a very loud belch. Several of his disciples must have felt that this was a significant belch, because as a body they prostrated themselves at his feet. I remember feeling quite honoured to be the source of all this adoration.

I then travelled by boat to stay on an idyllic, tropical island. I love islands and everything about this island was perfect; the ocean, the palm trees, the food and the company. Yet I remember feeling profoundly depressed in the middle of this paradise. I wanted a sense of purpose and a project rather than being a spectator in life. My only inspiration was music. I had started singing lessons in Sydney and had bought a guitar, so this helped to pass the time. Once again though, as soon as the going got tough it was time move somewhere else; new faces and new adventures.

My next stop was the island of Samoa, at that time a relatively unspoiled island where most of the people still lived very simple lives, gathering fruit from the trees and fishing. I stayed overnight in the capital city and got up early to take the bus to the other side of the island. I was at first the only person in the bus and I waited and waited. Eventually people arrived, hordes and hordes of them and soon the bus was filled. And then more people climbed on and started sitting on top of the ones already seated. One young, rather attractive girl came and sat on my knee. There was nowhere else to sit.

With the two sisters from Samoa

And then another equally attractive girl, her sister as it turned out, came and sat on her knee and off we went through the jungle on a very bumpy dirt road. In spite of all my very best efforts to stay calm, I started to get sexually aroused, cringing with embarrassment, trying to wriggle around so that the girl on top wouldn't feel anything. She seemed quite unperturbed, perhaps she didn't even notice (what a cheek!) and then we started to chat. It turned out that her father who was sitting across the passageway was the chief of a tribe and he invited me to stay with the tribe.

I was given a royal reception on arrival and partook in a ceremony where I drank the locally brewed cava which gave a light but quite noticeable sense of wellbeing. My vegetarian diet proved to be a problem, more for them than for me because I would have been content to eat only fruit from the trees. They didn't grow vegetables and the chief insisted on going back into town and getting me a tin of peas. Life was very relaxed for everyone. It was hot and humid and so everyone would get up early, have a fruit breakfast, sit around and chat and then take a little nap. Then the men would go fishing and the women would prepare the fish when it eventually arrived. And so it went on. The highlight of the week was the screening of an American film in a big tent which I attended with the two sisters. It was all very innocent and I was treated with exceptional kindness.

My experience in Samoa gave me plenty of food for thought as I made my way back to Scotland via American Samoa, Honolulu and Montreal. I had experienced firsthand tribal living and although there were drawbacks it seemed to me that our souls crave this sort of connection with others. Maybe one day I would be able to recreate this sort of tribal experience.

SEVEN

CAMBRIDGE AND MENORCA

Once again, after spending only a few days with my family, the big question loomed; what to do with the rest of my life? Thinking about what most inspired me, I thought of music, and that very day I came across an advert for a one week singing course in the Welsh hills to take place the following week and so I made my way there. We were a small group of students and all day long we practiced singing excerpts from Mozart's Magic Flute. I came alive. It was a huge realisation, that I loved working in a group and performing. Suddenly and quite dramatically, I decided that I wanted to be an opera singer. It was a strange choice to make at the age of 28. Opera singers usually start training when they are in their teens and they normally have a good knowledge of music. My voice was good. It was a strong voice and I could sing in tune but it was not exceptional. My thinking was that with say, six or seven years hard work, I could be a professional singer and have a successful career. Enrolling in a course in music at The Music and Art College in Cambridge, I was advised to study music theory and to learn to play the piano.

Cambridge wasn't fun. It was freezing cold that winter with winds which seemed like they'd blown in straight from Siberia. Certainly there were beautiful ancient buildings and plenty of excellent concerts but it seemed to me to be a place of privilege, dominated by the ancient university of Cambridge; students (80 % of whom at that time were male) versus local people. But most of all, the music course that I was doing was very disappointing. I wanted to learn how to sing but I found my singing teacher self-centred and not really focused on my development. The main thrust of the course was music theory and piano playing rather than singing.

To cap it all, I was unhappy with my lodgings. I was staying in a room above the owners, an Indian family who kept to themselves. Everything seemed to reinforce the feeling that I was an outsider, missing out on something. Things got worse and worse and I started to feel depressed. I was constantly questioning why I had chosen to try to become an opera singer and whether it was a realistic choice.

One Sunday night, always the loneliest night of the week for me, things came to a head and I started to toy with the idea of killing myself. I was crying and feeling sorry for myself, angry at the Indian family downstairs who seemed to be ignoring me. I had a few drinks, hoping it would make me feel better. It didn't. I took a large knife from the kitchen and played with the idea of plunging it into my belly. Even in my inebriated state this proved impossible. I simply couldn't do it. I then had the idea of driving my car at speed into a wall. Good idea, I thought to myself, but its freezing cold outside. I lay in bed and thought about how to do it and then I had a brainwave. I would climb to the top of King's College (one of the University buildings nearby) and jump off. Great idea! But as I lay in bed I started to feel a little bit drowsy and I then had another idea. I'll do it in the morning when I'm fresh and ready, I said to myself. With that I started to relax and let go. Just before I went to sleep, I saw above me a light, as if it were two angelic hands blessing me. A few moments later I was fast asleep.

Waking up next morning I thought to myself, what the heck was all that about? I could still feel a little cloud of despair above my head but nothing like the previous evening. This cloud lasted for about a month but little by little I started to feel better about life and came to realise that on some level I was safe and protected.

I still wasn't sure about becoming an opera singer. Progress on the piano seemed very slow and my singing didn't seem to have improved. With hindsight I realised that even though I was living quite economically, the fact that I was receiving money from home to sustain me meant that my choices were too vast. Want to be an opera singer? Ok, just go ahead and learn. Fortunately the decision as to whether to continue was taken out of my hands. One of my brothers felt strongly that I should no longer take money from the family partnership to sustain my lifestyle and that I should work for my living. He did me a great service.

With no regrets I gave up my singing and music studies and got a job teaching yoga and doing massage in a naturopathic clinic. Tyringham Clinic was the brainchild of an east London Jew Sydney, Rose-Neill. It was in a huge Georgian mansion, set in twenty acres of beautifully manicured gardens near Milton Keynes, one hour north of London. I taught yoga and aqua gym (pool exercises) and sometimes I gave massages. It was a sort of honey pot for a young man with lots of attractive women coming every week. I lived on the top floor of the mansion and as we were not supposed to fraternise with the guests, the element of danger added a certain frisson to the encounters. Every Friday evening (their last night) I was allowed to mix with the guests to organise a cabaret. Again I was in my element, as I loved to perform. On one occasion I sang the Mozart aria (Non Piu Andrai) accompanied on the piano by the well known conductor Sir Charles Mackeras. Another frequent visitor was the famous singer Cleo Lane whom I had the pleasure of massaging. After about six months, with winter approaching, I began to feel restless. My main source of inspiration was the guests and they changed every week. I longed for stability and to have more purpose in life.

The wages at Tyringham were very poor and when another staff member suggested that we all join a trade union to push for higher wages, I enthusiastically took up the cause. I recruited most of my fellow workers to join the Transport and General Workers Union, a notoriously left-wing organisation. The management was incensed and I was called upon to explain myself. However, with the power of the Union behind me, they were not in a position to discipline me. They gave a quite substantial increase in wages and lobbied for us to join a more moderate union. This rather took the wind out of my sails. I didn't particularly like politics and confrontation and I retired from my position of Union organiser. Gradually things went back to normal.

Becoming more and more discontented with my life I started to look for a project to dedicate myself to. A lot of wealthy clients passed through Tyringham, all of them with an interest in natural health. After one or two false starts, a client named Maurice Newbound proposed that I develop his property in Menorca, in the Balearic Islands, as a health clinic. I spoke Spanish and my task was to do odd maintenance jobs and supervise a building project. The property was in a valley in the centre of Menorca, near the town of Alayor. Maurice was a wealthy, self-made man who always drove a hard bargain and yet I was very fond of him. I had never done any practical building work before. In my dad's factory I wasn't even allowed to pick up a sack of grain. "Darling," my dad would say, "we have workers to do that." So it was a steep learning curve for me. I did my best to tidy the place up but it was very hot and I didn't find labouring in the garden on my own an easy task.

I was feeling lonely and not enjoying being in the house. It was quite isolated and in a valley and it always felt kind of spooky and perhaps even haunted when I would go home in the evenings. Luckily I made one or two friends locally and they helped me in the garden so that when Maurice came on one of his periodic visits, he was quite impressed with the progress made. Unfortunately he discovered my marijuana plants that I'd been carefully grooming. I had danced and prayed around these plants and was sure they were of the highest quality. Maurice ripped them out in disgust and threw them on the compost. Very luckily I was able to recuperate them when he had gone and as I had expected it was the best marijuana I had ever smoked.

We hired a team of builders to do some major renovation work and my task was to ensure that the work progressed as planned. The builders were very pleasant and conversational, even though there were enormous cultural differences. They knew a lot about subsistence farming and house maintenance but had had very little exposure to life as lived in the cities of Europe. The dictator Franco had just died and there was an explosion of freedom in Spain at that time. Many mystics, yogis and hippies arrived to settle around Alayor, near where I lived and they were viewed with a mixture of suspicion and curiosity by the locals.

On the rare occasions when I managed to persuade a woman to stay overnight with me, the workers made all kinds of excuses to come and take a peak when my visitor was using the outside shower. One worker Emiliano was delighted to be served mint tea by a lovely naked Italian lady Rosina and he told me afterwards that it had inspired him to co-create a second child with his wife.

Maurice's visits became more and more strained. He was an obsessive worker and insisted on the same level of dedication from me. I was earning a pittance and slowly started to become dissatisfied with the situation. The building project was going ahead well enough and I realised that there was no need for me to continue.

Resigning from my position I spent the next couple of months living in a VW van, lent to me by some travellers from Brazil. I would sleep in a different place every night, always on the top of a hill, as the van had a problem with the starting motor. I felt very at home with the young travelling people who had settled in the area. They were creative and idealistic and had come to the island to create a different sort of lifestyle. I survived by teaching English and doing a bit of massage.

At one point I brought a suitcase with clothes and jewellery from the UK which had been imported from India, at a very low cost and I sold them on the main street in Barcelona, Las Ramblas. I was doing extremely well until I was arrested and taken to the police station in a police van with other delinquents. We each paid a small fine and went straight back to the street to sell more. It was the 5th of January, the day before Three Kings Day when Spanish traditionally gave each other presents. They were buying my stock up at such a rapid rate that it was too good an opportunity to miss. I kept one eye open for the police and eventually managed to sell up all my stock and return to Menorca relatively rich.

It would have great to have stayed on the island but unfortunately it was not to be. It was impossible to rent a house at a reasonable price and I didn't feel like living in a van with a broken starting motor and very little money forever. With a heavy heart I left the island and made my way back to the UK.

EIGHT

PORTSMOUTH POLYTECHNIC

I felt that I had hit rock bottom. It seemed to me that I had spent the last seven years going round in circles. I hadn't found the illumination I was seeking nor had I found purpose in my life. I was tired of having very little money and was starting to feel that somehow I had failed in the eyes of my family. I was staying in a chic part of London with my cousin Alan Yentob who was already a successful BBC producer. We had been very close when we were younger and now he had money and status whilst it seemed to me that I had very little. He was incredibly kind and he let me stay rent free for six months whilst I found my feet.

Doing odd jobs to survive I eventually started a business, importing novelty jewellery boxes from my cousin in California. It wasn't something that I was particularly cut out for and my heart wasn't really in it although it did reasonably well for a time.

When I started to apply for jobs I very quickly realised that I was virtually unemployable except for pretty basic work. How was I going to explain seven years of travelling without stable work? One of my cousins suggested that I make up a CV saying that I had worked in Australia for my cousin Charlie. I had stayed with Charlie and his family on numerous occasions. He was a wonderfully kind man with a very successful fabrics business in Sydney.

I invented a job for myself with Charlie; a job which would suit my legitimate credentials, an Honours degree in Economics and a Masters degree in Marketing. These were considered to be excellent qualifications in those days. I applied for the prestigious post of Senior Lecturer in Marketing at Portsmouth Polytechnic and was asked to come for an interview a fortnight later. It was extremely well paid work, especially as I had been subsisting on a near pittance. My story was that I was the Marketing Director in Charlie's firm and had 6 salesmen reporting directly back to me from different parts of Australia. I supervised sales targets and implemented advertising and marketing strategies and of course was paid an enormous salary for such an important job! I had had a very successful career, climbing the ranks from salesman to head salesman, eventually after four years being appointed Marketing Director.

Sometime later I came across a book about how to succeed at interviews. I pressed my suit and cut my hair. It was vital to look the part. I found out all that I could about the job and rehearsed my lines in front of the mirror. I asked my mother to pray for me knowing that she believed in the power of prayer and was very anxious for me to succeed.

The day of the interview arrived. I travelled by train from London to Portsmouth. I was to go before an interview panel of four, which included the Vice Chancellor of the Polytechnic as well as the head of the Business Studies Department. I took a little sip of vodka before the interview to hone my acting skills. I was magnificent! I lived my job and it was convincing. I was offered the job on the spot with apologies that it was nothing like what I had been earning in Australia. I accepted graciously, saying that I had reached a point in my career where teaching and research were more important than making money.

"Subject of course," said the Vice Chancellor, "to your reference from Australia being satisfactory."

And so I travelled back to London in a state of great excitement. I phoned my mother to tell her the good news.

"Oh Nigel," she said. "I love you." The words just slipped out. My mother's generation never expressed emotions but I was delighted with her response nevertheless. Next I phoned Charlie in Australia to ask him to write me a reference. "I already have," he replied.

My heart sank. "And what did you say?"

"I told them that you were a really nice guy and that you had once worked for me for a couple of days."

Oh fuck, I thought. "Look Charlie," I said. "There is a bit of a problem here but I will get back to you." I didn't want to say too much until I had found some sort of solution.

That night I drank whisky. I rarely drink in desperation but I was in dire straits. I was especially concerned about my mother. I talked to one of my cousins. "Look," he suggested, "why don't you say that when you were in Australia you called yourself Rodger?" This was the truth as it happens and then he continued, "You had this cousin called Nigel who was a useless sort of bugger and now that you are Nigel again, your employer obviously got confused and wrote a reference about the wrong person." Not very convincing but worth a try as I couldn't think of anything better. I didn't sleep well that night. I prayed with great passion. Next morning I phoned up the Staff Department of the Polytechnic and spoke to a woman called Paula. "Have you received the reference from Australia yet?" I inquired.

"Funny you should call but I just received it this morning."

"Have any of the interviewing panel seen it yet?"

"No," she replied, "but I was just about to show it to them."

"Look, can you just hold on for a while? There is something I need to explain to you."

"That's fine," she replied agreeably.

And so I hopped on a train, still in my best suit, and made my way to Portsmouth and to Paula's office. She turned out to be a sweetheart. I explained my story to her about the misunderstanding made by my employer.

"Oh fine," she replied. "Do you want me to tear it up?" I couldn't believe my ears.

This was going incredibly well. "If you don't mind," I replied.

"Well, make sure that you get a proper reference this time." And that was that.

I went back to London and gave my cousin Charlie a call, explaining that I needed a different sort of reference.

"I don't like doing this," he said "but I will do it for you." Thank God he was so fond of me. "Write to me, telling me exactly what to say."

And so I did. However the saga continued. There was a postal strike in Australia. This was well before the days of the internet. The job was to start in 4 weeks time.

I hung on tenterhooks waiting for the strike to end. I was fairly confident about teaching marketing even though it had been years since I had studied it. It's a bit of a bla bla subject often based on anecdotal references which has been given importance because it is so vital in the modern world of consumerism. There was a standard reference book on the subject which I studied before the job was to begin.

The day before I started work, I went again to see Paula in the Staff Department.

"Has the letter arrived from Australia yet?" I asked.

"You are in luck" she replied. "It arrived just a couple of days ago."

And so began my career as a Senior Lecturer in Marketing. I tended to avoid the other teachers in the Business Studies Department. Remember, I had to pretend I had had a highly successful career in marketing. But more than that, I didn't have much in common with them.

However I loved my contact with the students, so fresh and enthusiastic. I loved to entertain them with funny stories about marketing. Above all I told them not to take marketing too seriously. I didn't want them studying too much of that stuff!

Above: With my French studies marketing students

Below: Laughter game with students

With some of my classes I had a secret sign which meant, "Listen up! You will get a question about this in the exam." I made up the exam questions and also marked the papers so I made sure that the results were good but not too good. As I write I'm thinking it was all highly unethical but I really wanted them to have fun and also to have another perspective about the concept of marketing. I remember hosting a party for all my Engineering students doing a marketing option (all boys) and all my French Studies marketing students (all women). They were all a bit shy at first but I got them to break the ice with a laughter game where they all lay on the floor and placed their heads on each others' bellies. I was beginning to realise that laughter was a much better ice breaker than alcohol.

My French Studies students were my favourites. I told them one week that the colours they were wearing were dull and I wanted them to come to the lecture wearing something red. The next week it was yellow. The following week they were to wear at least one item of fancy dress. I turned up with a false nose and a little yellow hat perched on the top of my head. When I opened the door, I saw that they had arranged the desks so that it looked like a director's board room. All of them had false noses and weird clothes. We looked at each other and laughed so hard and for so long that a science teacher who was lecturing next door burst into the room without knocking.

"Very funny!" he said angrily, "but I'm trying to teach next door."

This was even funnier because we had to laugh without making a noise. This went on and on. I eventually tried to start the lecture, more laughter, until mercifully the bell rang. We all felt fantastic. This was a great lesson for me in later life as I started to incorporate laughter into my yoga and Chi Kung classes.

The work was incredibly easy the first year. Higher level teaching in those days was very stress free. We were encouraged to do research and publish papers but nobody said anything if you didn't. It was a job for life with a good salary unless you did something badly wrong, which leads me to my next story...

I was living in a terraced house with three students who were renting rooms from me. One evening there was a knock on the door. There were six policemen and a dog looking for drugs.

"Ok, Sir," said the chief officer. "Tell us where the drugs are before we take the place apart."

I had a tiny bit of marijuana left and I showed it to them. They searched around for a while (one of my tenants had the presence of mind to quickly flush his drugs down the toilet) and found nothing else. It's strange, the reaction caused by fear. I felt a sort of cold, hollow feeling in my stomach, very unpleasant. I was scared I would lose my job. Worse than that, they might investigate my past and find out the truth. How would my mother take all this? What was ironic was that I had been to India a few weeks before and had been so impressed by my encounter with the guru Sai Baba that I had resolved to stop smoking marijuana in the near future. The police had all come straight from the pub. They smelled strongly of alcohol and it felt like an invasion. They took me to the police station where they went through the usual charging procedures and I was summoned to appear before the court a few days later.

I realised why they had come. One week previously the police had made a house to house search looking for a rapist. They had smelled the incense, seen the pictures of gurus on the wall and students lounging around and they figured that we must be doing drugs.

"Okay, Sai Baba, my new friend," I prayed. "Get me out of this one."

The court hearing went well enough. I told the judge it was just a little experiment, that I had not shared it with any of the students and that I was very sorry. I was given a fairly hefty fine.

Later that day to my horror, the story appeared in the local paper, The Portsmouth Evening News, "Polytechnic Lecturer Might Lose His Job." The students were very supportive and some of them threatened to go on strike were I to lose my job. I knew my career was very much in the balance. I was summoned before the Chancellor to explain myself. He told me off in no uncertain terms and let me know that he had informed the Ministry of Education in London. I received a letter from the Home Secretary himself to the effect that he was very disappointed in my behaviour but that after due reflection, I would be able to keep my job if I could get 6 people of high standing to vouch for my good behaviour. That was not a problem. I had plenty of friends of high standing. And so I continued to teach, rising in the esteem of the students and falling in the esteem of some members of the Business Studies Department.

Forty years later I am pondering whether my actions were highly immoral. I don't advocate telling lies but I knew at the time that I could do the job well. The students loved my classes and in my opinion they got a deeper insight into the world of marketing than they would have got with a more conventional teacher. So to some extent the end justified the means.

NINE

SAI BABA AND PREMANANDA

It's 1980 and I'm well established in my new job at Portsmouth Polytechnic in a new home, close to the sea. I was still doing yoga every day but it felt like time to have new inspiration. I decided to find a guru. So many of my generation were heading to Pune to see Rajneesh later known as Osho, some attracted by his libertine approach to sexuality others by his excellent writings, lectures and teaching methods. But there was something about him that I didn't like. Why did he permit himself to be gifted so many Rolls Royces? It didn't add up and I didn't trust him.

My friend Julia had been to see Sai Baba and she talked highly of him. He was a tiny man in his 50's with an Afro hairstyle and a long orange robe. He was born in Puttaparthi near Bangalore in southern India and since an early age he had been displaying miraculous yogic powers. He was apparently telepathic, an amazing healer and he could even materialize objects out of thin air. He also did a lot of charitable work and was in the process of building hospitals and schools, financed by wealthy donors. It was said that even Indira Gandhi would consult with him on important matters of state. His teaching was simple; be good, do good and love one another. Apparently he had transformed the lives of millions of his followers.

That Christmas I decided to fly to India to see him. I was not alone. When, after a long harrowing journey, I arrived at his ashram, there was a huge throng of people who had come for the Christmas celebrations. I was offered shelter in an enormous bare corrugated iron shed. There was only a thin threadbare mattress on the concrete floor. I was so tired that sleep came immediately. I was rudely awoken at 4 a.m. the next morning by horrific noises. Indians have a custom of noisily clearing their throats first thing in the morning and when you have over 100 of them doing it all at once in a corrugated iron shed, the noise is astounding. Reluctantly I got up and went for meditation and breakfast. The ashram was run like an army camp by volunteers who seemed to revel in their positions of authority and would tell us to hurry up, to slow down, to keep quiet or whatever took their fancy. It was extremely crowded and it wasn't pleasant.

The highlights of the day were the two occasions when Sai Baba would come out of his temple and walk in front of the devotees who were sitting on the ground, the men on one side and the women on the other. The whole procedure would take less than 15 minutes as he took letters from some, talked briefly to others and materialized sacred ash for the lucky ones out of his bare hands. The luckiest of the lucky, usually about twenty out of the thousands of people assembled, were summoned for a private interview.

He generally chose people to come for an interview who were sitting at the front and there was tremendous competition for those places, involving hours of queuing in the hot sun. For most people the end goal was to have an interview with him, even if it were only once in a lifetime. I never managed to get near the front and he never looked my way. I hated the crowds, the noise and the petty officials and after four days I decided that I would leave and visit Rajneesh (Osho) instead. At least I would have a lot of fun there. However, I decided to spend my last night in prayer, asking for an interview and his blessing. But I was exhausted and ultimately fell asleep. By the time I woke up, it was too late to get in the queue to ensure a front seat. I dressed and got in the queue anyway. I'm not sure how it happened but the row I was queueing in seemed to get preference and I ended up managing to get a seat in the third row from the front.

I decided that after coming this enormous distance, I was at least going to beg for an interview. I was planning to get up off the floor, throw myself at his feet and beg for him to listen to me and give me his blessing. I knew I would get into severe trouble with all his bouncers and assistants but I felt lost and desperate. At last Baba walked by. I was just about to make my dramatic gesture when he looked up at me.

"You're leaving today?" he asked.

"Yes," I replied.

"Come inside." He pointed to where I was to go.

I was elated. I felt as if I had won the jackpot. A few minutes later about twenty of us assembled in a small room inside the temple. Baba appeared. He was very small and very charming. There was an air of tremendous excitement in the room. Baba started performing miracles. Holy ash came pouring out of his hand for some; for another he made a gold ring which fitted his finger exactly. I'm convinced there was no trickery. I'm not sure if I imagined it but I had the impression that there was a glowing energy that came out of his hand as he made the ring.

He would select families and talk to them privately in an adjoining room for a short while. They would come out, looking happy and excited. Finally it was my turn. I was amazed at how small he was, this man who had such power and influence. He talked about himself in the third person.

"You have been worried and upset, thinking that Baba doesn't know you…but Baba knows everything."

He told me to kneel.

"Now I will bless you. Now you can go." And off I went, delighted and happy that I had indeed been chosen by this diminutive man who seemed to have such a big heart.

Outside I was like a rock star.

"What happened? What did he say?"

But I wasn't keen to talk too much. I had said I was going and it felt like time to go. I visited another guru in Bangalore out of curiosity. He was said to have attained miraculous powers by standing on one leg for thirteen years as an act of penance and was now crippled. He was a very interesting man but I didn't feel anything like the strong attraction I had felt for Baba. A few days later Baba came to Bangalore where I was staying and I got another chance to see him. As he was passing, he gazed up at me and spent what seemed like a long time, looking at me, thinking I know not what. Again I felt a surge of joy and a feeling that I had been understood.

And so I returned to Portsmouth. I was anxious to meet other people there who knew of him but sadly nobody had heard of him except my friend Julia. A few days after my return, another friend Robin told me that he had seen an advert on the window of a newsagent's shop, publicising a meeting being organised by some devotees of Baba about his life and teachings

Early the next morning I got up to investigate but on the way there I had to stop by the side of the road because I had got something stuck in my tooth. I looked up. There was a huge picture of Baba. I had stopped outside the Spiritualist Church where a meeting was to take place the following Saturday. It was the first time such a meeting had taken place in Portsmouth and it was to happen within a week of my returning from India. I felt tremendously excited that even at this vast distance he could make his presence felt. This was not a "normal" human being.

Baba is very popular with the Indian community in the UK and a group of his devotees did a presentation of Baba's work that Saturday, showing a video of him performing miracles and blessing his devotees. They sang a couple of devotional songs in Sanskrit, accompanied by a harmonium and two drums called *tablas*. After a short speech one of them asked if anyone wanted to say anything and so I got up and told my story. I suggested that if anyone were interested, we could meet at my house on a weekly basis to sing devotional songs and to meditate. There seemed to be a flurry of interest but this was new territory for most of them. Their interest up to now had been mainly channelling messages from the dead and spiritual healing.

To my delight seven or eight people turned up and soon I had a regular, weekly group meeting. We sang devotional songs in Sanskrit, we meditated and we had philosophical discussions over tea and cakes. We all felt that we had been blessed in some special sort of way. All of them eventually made individual life changing trips to see Baba and were all so enthusiastic that soon we extended the meetings to twice weekly. I made two more trips to see Baba but I was never called for an interview again.

My mother visited around this time and I could tell she wasn't too impressed with the pictures of Baba plastered all over the wall. It was very much against the Jewish tradition to have any images of any type of god, least of all a human being. But discreet as always, she said very little.

After about eighteen months I started to feel as if I were treading water with Baba. I longed for a more personal contact with a teacher. Somebody told me of a young guru in Sri Lanka, called Premananda. He had apparently all the same powers of healing, clairvoyance and manifestation as Baba and it was possible to get very close to him as he was not yet inundated with followers.

I had been dating a fellow devotee of Baba, called Catherine and we were thinking of getting married. I wasn't in love with her but I was trying to live the spiritual life, no alcohol, no drugs, no partying and I felt lonely. I thought that to be with a fellow devotee would be a match made in heaven. We travelled to Sri Lanka together to meet Premananda to get his blessing for our marriage. He was wonderfully charismatic and I was hugely attracted right from the beginning. He seemed like a younger version of Baba with the same tiny stature, the bushy Afro hairdo and the same flowing orange robes. He fitted the bill for the teacher I had been looking for. He was young, funny and playful and I loved the atmosphere of his ashram. Sometimes we would have water fights, drenching each other with water. Premananda would caution us never to mention any of our horse play to anyone outside the ashram. Sri Lanka was a conservative country and outside the ashram he played a very different character.

He looked like a guru and played the part well. He would keep the public waiting but when he did finally appear it was with a grand entrance with one or two miraculous manifestations of holy ash (just like Baba). He would then sing a couple of Sanskrit chants sending the crowd into ruptures. There was a certain chemistry in the air at these public events. Premananda would send out his love and blessings to the crowd and they would return it to him tenfold. Everyone there felt that it was a huge blessing, simply to witness the event.

He had a wonderful companion, a retired gentleman called Shiva who had been the government's Chief Engineer. Shiva translated for Premananda and generally acted as his spokesman. I loved Premananda and all the people around him. There were five other westerners who lived in the ashram, all highly intelligent, affectionate people. Premananda blessed Catherine and I and told us we could get married, simple as that. I cringe as I write this. I was so lost, that I was prepared to get married for the rest of my life just because I was lonely and the guru had told me it was okay.

I introduced Catherine to my mother and family a couple of months later. They were unimpressed. My mother in particular realised that this was not a marriage based on love. I started to have frequent arguments with Catherine. And yet we arranged that she would give up her job in Switzerland and come and live with me in Portsmouth. What was I thinking of? I'd come little by little to accept the traditional Indian idea that the guru would lead me to God. Just before she arrived I started to get involved with another woman and it was slowly dawning on me that marriage to Catherine might not be such a good idea. And yet, Premananda had told me that it would be a good marriage and with his divine powers he should know. I phoned him and with Shiva translating I told him it wasn't working out with Catherine and asked if he could confirm that I should go ahead with the marriage. He advised me not to get married. I'm wondering as I write this, how I could have accepted that one day he says yes, get married and later he says, no don't bother; very strange.

And so I called off the marriage. My mother was delighted. She had been extremely worried about me. Later that year I was very excited when Premananda came to visit the UK. He came to stay in my home in Portsmouth and met all the followers from my Sai Baba group who were still meeting faithfully twice a week. He later went up to Scotland and my mother went to visit him. She was unimpressed but again said very little. By then I was completely under his spell. I made two more trips to visit him and I decided to quit my job and go and live in his ashram. I was convinced that by going to live with him, living the spiritual life in the ashram, I would find everlasting peace. None of my colleagues at the Polytechnic understood my decision but the job meant very little to me by then. I was living a lie, teaching marketing which was in certain respects the very opposite of what I believed in. My students were very disappointed although one or two were curious about my decision and wanted to know more. I left Portsmouth in a state of great excitement eager for the next phase of my life.

It was strange being in the ashram on a full time basis. I had expected there would be a certain discipline; that we would learn various yogic techniques that would open us up to the Divine; nothing of the sort. We westerners were paraded in front of his many disciples to validate his reputation. I was introduced to the public as a learned professor. I suppose I looked the part. By this time I had gone native. I had a long flowing beard and wore the long, traditional *dhoti*, a sort of skirt like garment. The thing I enjoyed most was singing devotional chants and there were frequent opportunities to sing to the devotees. Premananda would seduce us with tales of how his special devotees would find everlasting peace, just what we wanted to hear.

Another highlight was the full moon ceremony when we would stay up all night. Premananda would go into a trance and would give his devotees words of advice, usually about matters of marriage, wealth and health. Sometimes he would be fierce and beat the ground with a stick.

"Why do you do this?" I asked. "Surely with all your powers you don't need to go into a trance."

"It's all a drama," he replied. "People love drama"

My roommate was Archie. He was a lot older than me, of Armenian descent. He was very laid back, sometimes annoyingly so. He had had a chequered career as a bouncer in a nightclub, a poker player and finally a drug dealer. One full moon evening we went for a very long walk and he told me the story of his life, how he used marked cards to cheat at poker and how once it led to him being severely beaten up. He eventually made a lot of money dealing in cannabis. He was second in command in a line of dealers. His boss was called "The Nose" and they would occasionally have meetings in a posh hotel. It was all cloak and dagger stuff. They would whisper to each other while splashing around in the pool, things like, "the deal is on" or, "send 50 kg of hash to Prakash in Delhi." If for example the fourth person in the chain got caught, the third person in the chain would be sent for a long paid holiday. Archie made a huge amount of money but he gave a lot of it away. He would hand it out to astonished beggars in the street. Becoming more discontented with his life, he found his way to Premananda and had an epiphany, deciding there and then to give him his money and become a disciple.

I loved Archie. It was comforting to me that other westerners that I respected so much were following Premananda. All of them had given him money, sometimes considerable sums and I, likewise gave him some of the money I had inherited from my dad. I had always felt that I should give away some of this money which had in part come from poultry farming. One of the Unit Trusts that I had bought almost doubled in value and I was able to give him a generous donation, more generous than I had intended. Although he didn't seem attached to money, he had a certain way of attracting it, lots of it. I too was pretty unattached to the money but years later when I was living in Spain and desperate for money to finance the project I was involved with, I very much regretted the size of this donation. I also felt a little guilty that I had given away my father's hard earned cash.

Little by little I grew tired of Premananda's erratic behaviour. We would be going somewhere early next morning and then we weren't. He would say one thing and then do another. I became sceptical of the act he put on for local devotees. Why does he do this, I thought? Most of all I didn't feel a trace more enlightened than when I set off from Portsmouth. And so I decided to tour around Sri Lanka on my own. I hadn't formally left the ashram but I knew I was heading in that direction.

The day that I left, tension had suddenly broken out between the Sinhalese, the original inhabitants of Sri Lanka who were Bhuddist and the Tamils who were Hindus. The Tamils had been imported from India by the British two centuries earlier to work the tea plantations, as they had proven to be much harder workers than the local Sinhalese. The Tamils were mostly in the northern and eastern parts of the island but there was a considerable minority in Matali in the centre of the island where I was staying. I was astonished! One day there had been peace and cooperation between the two communities and the next day mayhem. The tension in the air was palpable. People were scurrying around in all directions, shouting and crying. Many Tamils were being arrested. By a curious twist of fate I managed to catch the last bus out of town.

I eventually made my way to the naval port of Trincomalee in the eastern part of the island, where I stayed in a lovely hostel by the sea. The government had imposed a 6 p.m. curfew to quell what was now a civil war between the Sinhalese and the Tamils. I had been passing the time with a couple of young women, one from Scotland and one from France. We were feeling cooped up and a bit frustrated and one evening we went for a walk along the beach. After a few minutes we were confronted by a very large policeman carrying a gun.

"Sir, what are you doing here?" he asked.

He was polite but he looked menacing. As the male of the party all his attention was directed towards me. I acted innocent, saying that we didn't know anything about the curfew. We were taken to the police station and told to wait. Curfew breaking was a serious offence. I saw the officer who had apprehended us violently pulling an elderly lady by the ear. One of the girls with me looked terrified. I played the part of the strong male but I was scared. I had heard about Sri Lankan jails and there was a huge amount of tension in the air. I prayed. We waited and waited and I prayed some more. One of the girls was growing more and more miserable by the minute. Eventually the officer returned.

"Sir, this is very, very bad. You must never do this again." And so we were allowed to go home.

I returned to the ashram in Matali. Premananda was a Tamil as were most of his devotees and the ashram (which I had partly financed) had been burned to the ground together with many of my possessions. There was not much left of it. The Sinhalese were nothing if not thorough in their destruction. They were in theory Buddhists but this had nothing to do with Buddhism. It was pure jealousy and racism. The Tamils were equally violent in their reaction. This was a "lose lose" situation. I managed to recover a very charred notebook which had been precious to me. Most of the devotees and the western followers had been interred in a camp locally. I went to visit them and they told me how Premananda had escaped to India fearing for his life, and was planning another ashram there.

I was no longer particularly interested in him or any other guru for that matter. And neither were any of the other western devotees. We had all grown disillusioned, some more than others. The ones who had invested most of their energies in following him were the most disappointed. One girl from Germany who had been an ardent follower for some years told me that he had made the wife of one of his devotees pregnant. He was supposedly a celibate monk.

"Can you forgive your guru?" he asked.

"No," she replied simply.

And so we all went our separate ways. Archie went back to London where he started working as a taxi driver. He had started to smoke cannabis again, heavily. How he ever found his way around London I will never know. I didn't want to stay in a country in a state of civil war. There was no knowing how the situation would develop and so two days later I left Sri Lanka and made my way to South India ready for more adventures.

TEN

TRAVELS IN INDIA

I arrived in India from Sri Lanka at the beginning of 1984. I had no particular plan, no particular place to go. This felt a bit scary. I liked having plans and projects and in addition I was scared of catching some horrible stomach bug.

I visited Premananda. He was staying near Chennai with a well known American yoga teacher, Indra Devi. I stayed a couple of nights with him but for me the magic had gone. I paid one last visit to Sai Baba's ashram. There was growing evidence that he was a paedophile and that some of his materialisations were fake. I wasn't sure about this and I'm still not sure. I am convinced however that the miracles I saw were genuine. I concluded that sometimes a showman such as Baba feels that he has to perform miracles whether it comes naturally or not. I imagine that sometimes it was easier to fake it. In any event the materialisations, the healing, the bi-location and all the other myriad powers that he displayed made very little difference to me personally. He certainly had special powers but I was still me with my insecurities and lack of direction. It was the end of an era. I was sick of chasing gurus. It seemed to me that the guru disciple relationship where the disciple surrenders his will to the guru had by now served its purpose. We all had to find that inner light, that inner guru rather than rely on a physical teacher. Yes, we can seek out the company of inspiring friends to help us, plus books, videos and teachers but ultimately we have to rely on ourselves.

I made my way to the beautiful hill station of Kodaikanal which had been built by the British to escape the heat of the Indian summer. I felt very at home there. After what had been a break of several years I smoked some marijuana, with dramatic results. I started to feel ecstatically happy and had a vision of a white dome and a sense of falling in love. Oh great! I thought; a new lover. Just the job! I headed north to Delhi where I knew there was a famous temple with a dome. I was disappointed. No new visions. No new lover. I remembered that back in Kodaikanal I had met a young American David, who insisted that I must visit the Taj Mahal but that I must do it on the full moon.

I was very averse at that time to visiting tourist locations but David had been most insistent about it. Full moon was as it happens the next day and so the following morning I made my way to Agra, the home of the Taj Mahal. The train journey was supposed to take four hours but by the end of eight hours we still hadn't arrived and I was beginning to wonder if I'd ever get there for the full moon. I was so exasperated that I am ashamed to say that I got up and announced angrily to nobody in particular,

"This is a crazy country. Why can't you get your trains to run on time?"

Nobody said anything. They were all masters of the waiting game and for them this delay was no big deal. The train stopped and the three young schoolboys sitting opposite me got off the train. Just before we left one of the boys came running back onto the train and with a shy smile, slipped a bunch of bananas into my hand. It was a humbling experience. Once more I was in love with India.

We finally arrived in Agra. I checked into my hotel, showered, smoked a small joint and made my way by rickshaw to the Taj Mahal. I had not done any research about the building. All I remembered was a large white dome. I paid my money and entered a palace. It was extremely beautiful. It wasn't what I had expected. I couldn't see where the dome could be but still I was awestruck. Unbeknown to me this was only an entry palace, not the Taj itself. Just then I looked through a huge doorway and there glowing incandescently before me was the Taj Mahal. It was so feminine, like the most beautiful breast you could ever imagine. It was love at first sight. I cried and cried and kept saying,

"It's so beautiful, it's so beautiful." I seemed to be having a conversation with it. It beckoned me closer and I went inside.

Someone with a turban on his head was sitting chanting the sacred *om* in a deep baritone voice. The Taj is a wonderful echo chamber and I heard the echo of the echo of the echo and it seemed as if time had ceased to exist. Earlier I had briefly met some attractive American girls who were also visiting the Taj. I stood up hoping to get to know them better and quite abruptly banged my head. Again the building seemed to be talking to me.

"No stay here! You have much to learn."

And so the night went on. Yes, I had fallen in love but not with a woman. It was reassuring to know that this particular love would never go away. I stayed for hours gazing in rapture at the dome and its four minarets with the River Yamuna in the background.

I later found out that the Taj Mahal had been built in the 17th century by the Mogul emperor Shah Jehan to house the tomb of his favourite wife, Mumtaz Mahal. I felt comforted to know that the impulse for creating this architectural wonder had been love. Shah Jehan planned to build a replica in black marble on the other side of the river but unfortunately his son deposed and imprisoned him in a castle on the other side of the river and he died gazing at his masterpiece.

After a very short sleep I returned to Delhi in a fever of happiness and excitement. Later that day I boarded a train. I was on my way to Dharamsala, the home of the Dalai Lama, and a Mecca for spiritual seekers of all kinds. As I found my cabin, a very well dressed young man, wearing a purple turban politely asked if he could assist me, lifting my rucksack and guitar onto the luggage rack. Soon he was gone and the train took off. Suddenly I thought, where's my handbag? This is a small bag in which I carried all my valuables. Then, the bastard! He's taken it. It had all my travellers' cheques and my passport in it. I leapt to my feet and sought out the guard.

"Stop the train immediately!" I yelled.

"No Sir, that is not possible. You have to wait till the next stop in 30 minutes."

"Stop!" I yelled again. What was the point of heading further north without funds or passport. He was a big man but I pushed my weight against him.

"Stop immediately!" I said.

"No Sir. This is very bad. Be calm."

And so I took a big breath and calmed myself down. I even apologised for my behaviour. It wasn't his fault after all and there was little point stopping in the middle of nowhere. I got off at the next station about fifty miles north of Delhi.

I was exhausted and needed somewhere to sleep and I didn't want to spend any of the precious cash that I had kept in my pocket and which luckily had not been stolen. I went up to the first man I saw on the street, briefly told him my story and told him that I simply have to stay in his house. This was not at all my style. I'm usually quite hesitant about asking for favours but that night there were no holds barred. He seemed happy enough for me to sleep on his veranda. Early next morning I took a cheap train back to Delhi to report my missing passport to the British Embassy and to claim a refund for my stolen travellers' cheques. They told me that a refund would take nine days. There was no way around this. I would have to wait. I still had my train ticket to Dharamsala and I figured that if I lived very frugally, I might just about manage.

I ended up staying in the small town of McLoud Ganj, just above the palace of the Dalai Lama in Dharamsala. The next few days were some of the happiest of my life. I had very little money but I trusted in the universe. I was willing to receive whatever gifts might come my way and somehow I was well looked after. An American called Rick gave me some money for food. The hostel was very laid back and I could sometimes sneak in at night unbeknown to the owner and sneak out the next day without paying. The local Tibetans were lovely. They walked around the streets chanting their mantra *Om Mane Padme Hum* as they rolled their prayer beads. It was such a welcome change from the plains of India where westerners would be constantly assailed with demands to buy this or do that. The Tibetans seemed to have great respect for personal space unlike the Indians. I got to shake hands with the Dalai Lama. I remember fondly his twinkling eyes and hearty laugh; such a lovely man. I made up my mind there and then, never to trust a spiritual teacher who was unable to laugh heartily.

I teamed up with a lovely German doctor called Angelika. I was on a high for three whole days. Maybe this is the first step to enlightenment, I thought optimistically. No such luck. Angelika went off with another guy (she told me later she thought I wasn't interested). To cap it all, my financial situation was rapidly deteriorating. I returned back to the plains of India to spend time in a very cheap ashram before returning to Delhi to pick up my money. Rich again! Relieved and comforted to know I had the inner resources to survive this experience.

I travelled around for a while, making sure that I was back in Agra to experience the Taj Mahal at the next full moon. I was not disappointed. I had the same transcendent experience where I felt my heart opening with a deep love for family and friends. I spent a small fortune buying handcrafted carpets to send to my family. I went up to the desert oasis of Pushkar in Rajasthan and there I wrote long letters to all my family, but especially to my oldest brother Edward. Our relationship was a loving one but it had often been troubled and I wanted to pour my heart out, to apologise and explain some of the things I hadn't got right. It felt great to write even though 6 months later when I finally returned to the UK, none of my brothers or my mother felt able to even mention my letters. It didn't matter to me. The main thing was that they welcomed me home with open arms.

I spent the next few months visiting ashrams, temples and places of interest. In Rishikesh where the Beatles had studied meditation with Maharishi Mahesh Yogi, I saw an ascetic yogi in a trance, lying on a bed of long nails deeply embedded into his body. I took opium once in Rajasthan in an attempt to cure my diarrhoea. It didn't work very well but I did have the most amazing dreams that night. I spent time in Varanasi on the Ganges, famous for its *ghats* (funeral pyres) and one day I encountered a dead man in the middle of a pedestrian precinct. I touched him to see if he was really dead. He was. His body was still warm. I looked around for help but nobody took the slightest bit of notice. People came to Varanasi to die and it was considered a great blessing to do so. Later that day, I took a boat trip along the River Ganges. There were remains of human bodies floating by, whilst bathers would wash themselves enthusiastically in the sacred waters. *If you truly believe...*

In Calcutta I hung out with a well known filmmaker. He told me that he could make films more quickly than anyone else in the industry and that he would sometimes make three at once. He had a formula that his films always followed. Boy meets girl from a different caste, parents very angry, girl crying and boy sad, dance scene, mournful songs, parents finally relent, singing and dancing in celebration.

There was no internet in those days and international calls took hours to book and were prohibitively expensive. I communicated with long letters which usually took 10 days to arrive. Return letters were always sent to the Poste Restante of the post office of the town I was travelling to.

The noise was something that I never got used to. Earplugs were obligatory at night to dampen the sound of barking dogs, cocks crowing and the Muslim call to prayer at an ungodly hour of the morning. Occasionally I would get news of world events if I passed through a large town where they had newspapers. There were several excellent English language newspapers. Their style seemed quaint and archaic to my western ears. They were filled with words like dacoits (thieves), furlongs (220 yards) and lakhs (100.000). I liked reading the classified ads for wives advertising for husbands. I would tease my mum by sending her a cutting of a suitable bride and asking her opinion.

India is such a diverse country with many different cultures and languages. The people in the south are very dark and apparently have their roots in Africa whereas the people in the north are much fairer and they mostly originated in central Asia. There are also many different climatic regions and so as winter approached I started to travel south where it was warmer. I ended up at Shantivanam, 100 miles southeast of Chennai in Tamil Nadu. It was a Catholic monastery headed by a Benedictine monk from the UK, Father Bede Griffiths. The distinctive feature of the monastery was the use of local Hindu rituals in their search for the Divine. The meals were typically Indian, vegetarian and eaten on the floor in silence. It was Christmas time when I arrived and the monastery had attracted 20 - 30 spiritual seekers from all over the world.

I immediately made friends with two English guys, both musicians, and a German girl Rahmana who incidentally has remained a lifelong friend.

With my friend Rahmana in India

We would smoke a little marijuana together, play music and sing late into the night. We improvised a lot and Rahmana would dance. It was heaven. We put on a musical play for the community at Christmas. I was the compere and being a little bit stoned, I took the opportunity to ramble on in what I thought was an amusing way. The singing and dancing wasn't quite in the spirit of a Christian monastery but Father Bede could see that we had put a lot of work into it and he smiled benignly. He had a very open approach for someone steeped in the monastic tradition.

There was one young artist who used to smoke marijuana regularly. He had stopped smoking but he now had an artistic block. Father Bede advised him to take up smoking marijuana now and again to get the creative juices flowing again.

But there were rumblings of discontent. Word got around that we were playing music late into the night which was why we never made it to morning prayers. This was a monastery after all, dedicated to the contemplative life. Eventually Father Bede asked me to come to his little hut. He was perfectly charming. I could see why many of the residents treated him as a guru although it was not something that he ever encouraged. He asked me all sorts of questions about my life and what I hoped to do. Eventually he asked most delicately,

"Nigel, when do you think you might be moving on?"

" In two or three days," I answered.

"That's fine," he replied. "I really don't think this is the best place for you."

He was such a gentleman. He could have just as easily told me that I was a disruptive influence and that I should leave as soon as possible.

And so I continued my wanderings throughout southern India. The south is very different from the north of India. The people are calmer, they don't push and fight their way onto public transport and they are less invasive of your private space. They are better educated and they are fewer people chronically hungry. I enjoyed my travels, visiting different ashrams and holy sites. I particularly enjoyed the backwater trip in Alleppey, going through canals and rivers, looking at majestic scenery and watching people go about their daily lives.

Eventually I ended up in Goa. Now Goa is quite different to the rest of India. Goa had been a Portuguese colony up to the 1950's and most of the people had converted to Christianity. It was strange to see so many churches and so few temples. There were fewer vegetarian restaurants. I remember being in a toilet. This is disgusting, so please miss out the next paragraph if you are squeamish.

After I had finished my ablutions, I heard rumblings below and then a couple of satisfied grunts, as an enormous pig greedily devoured my offerings. It was the first pig I had seen in all my travels in India; camels, elephants, roosters, goats and lots of cows with bells wandering freely about but never a pig.

You're back, oh squeamish ones? Good. Anyway, Goa in 1984 was a seaside paradise, a haven for young people from all over the world who wanted to party. Mass tourism had not yet arrived and there were still many beaches where nudity or at the most a G-string was the order of the day. Occasionally there would be a busload of Indian tourists who had come to goggle at the sights. I wasn't happy here. Unlike other parts of India there was a lot of heavy drinking and noisy parties. I met very few spiritual seekers and I felt out of place. In addition I was starting to suffer from chronic diarrhoea.

I had been wandering around India for 8 months and I had been wondering if it were time to go home. I wasn't keen to go straight away. One of my best friends, Julia whom I had been writing to regularly, was getting married and many of my friends would be going. That very same day my nephew Andrew was having his Bar Mitzvah, an event not to be missed: maybe easier to stay a bit longer? And then I saw a bus trip advertised from Goa to Kathmandu in Nepal, visiting historic caves and exotic sites along the way, staying in pre-arranged, affordable lodgings at night. The journey was to take around 2 weeks.

It sounded wonderful. It turned out that most of my fellow travellers fitted the stereotype image of hippies; long-haired, anarchic and constantly stoned. The *chillum* or marijuana filled pipe would regularly make its way around the bus. Since I had arrived in Goa I had been smoking marijuana every night and I wasn't even getting particularly high. I looked at the other travellers. Many of them had hacking coughs and looked unhealthy. It was a bit of a wakeup call and I decided to severely limit my consumption of marijuana from then on.

The bus journey seemed endless. We visited the famous caves at Ajanta and also Osho's ashram in Pune. By now the guru had fled to Oregon but some of his many followers remained and I got a sense of his life and teachings.

There was me and three women in the bus who were not in the smoking club and we would hang out together. Our travelling companions seemed to be getting more and more discontent and argumentative. The smokers by now wanted to head straight to Kathmandu without stopping. Whilst that seemed an inviting prospect, our group of four knew we needed a good night's rest from time to time. And so, after a lot of heated discussion, a compromise was made. We would pick up the pace but there would be sleep times. Eventually, much to everyone's relief we made it to Kathmandu.

The people were very friendly. The restaurants catered to western tastes and there was a tolerance towards marijuana. It was no wonder that it had become over the years such a popular destination for so many people. And there were the mountains, beautiful, towering and majestic. None of these adjectives did them justice.

And to top it all, the rhododendron trees, yes trees, not bushes (like in Scotland) were in bloom. I went trekking on what was called Jonson Trail. I was still struggling with diarrhoea. Looking back I'm wondering why I didn't go to a doctor, get a stool test and take antibiotics. But strangely, nobody that I ever came across even suggested that. I tried various folk cures but nothing seemed to work. I struggled on. Climbing was tough, especially when we reached altitudes of over 12,000 feet and this made me even more tired. Often it was a case of one step at a time. I was eating mainly bananas, plain crackers and yoghurt which were said to be good for people with tummy issues. It was cold at night and exhausted, I would seek the warmth of my bed at 7 p.m., ready for a 5 a.m. start.

Soon I had had enough of Nepal. I wanted to do something about my health. I had heard that the Tibetans were good healers and I stopped in Dharamsala, the home of the Dalai Lama. I consulted a Tibetan doctor. He was well thought of and reputed to be the personal physician of the Dalai Lama. He was everything a doctor should be. He shook my hand warmly, asked a couple of questions, took my pulses (in the Tibetan system there are many pulses) and looked me up and down in silence for a while. He then presented me with three giant, black horse pills which I managed to swallow with great difficulty.

Miraculously I was cured and I felt ready to leave India and face life in the west.

I got a cheap ticket from Delhi to Athens. I had been so used to the hustle and bustle of India that Athens looked deserted. I spent a few days on the island of Hydra and made my way via Italy to Munich where Angelika, whom I'd met a few months earlier in McLoud Ganj lived. We had a lovely romantic time together for a while. She had a busy life as a doctor, a very possessive 6 year old son and an even more possessive dog called Wally and I couldn't see an easy future for us together.

Eventually it was time to head back to the UK. I was feeling more confident, more at peace with myself as if I had been through some sort of initiation and I was looking forward to the next stage of my life.

ELEVEN

FOLLOWING MY DREAM

I had spent a long time thinking about the idea of setting up a community somewhere in a warm climate. My idea was to do it with some like-minded souls. The only trouble was that I couldn't find people with similar ideas. This was before the days of the internet and Meetup groups. I spent the summer that year on the west coast of Ireland. I say "summer" but we only had two days of summer in the two months I was there. I remember being suspicious when I arrived in Dublin, one wet and windy day and people were saying to me, "Tis a grand day."

On the west coast of Ireland music and musicians were celebrated. I had a black hat and a gold stud in my left ear just to make sure that I looked like a musician. I'd walk into a pub, carrying my guitar and someone would say, "Give us a song, will ya." I'd start singing and soon they'd be a pint of Guinness by my side. I stayed in youth hostels. I have fond memories of a hostel on the island of Cape Clear. The manager had a face like a gnome and a twinkle in his eyes.

"We have to close the doors at 10 p.m. by law but if ye get delayed, I'll leave the window open for ye."

There were three pubs on the island. The first one closed at 10 p.m. and then we'd move on to the second one that closed at midnight and then to the third one that closed at 2 a.m. Such cooperation meant that all three pubs got their fair share of the trade. The pubs were all about the music. Everyone joined in and if they couldn't sing, they'd tell a story. One old weather-beaten man, with a cloth cap would tell the same story every night.

"Ye've missed a bit, Patrick," someone would yell.

Ireland is a wonderful country and I would have gladly settled there, but the constant rain finally got to me and I returned to the UK. I went to a community in Dorset called Monkton Wyld to do a five day Tai Chi course. We were in strict silence and though I spent a lot of my time and energy lusting after one of the female participants, I did get a lot out of the course. I'd wake up each morning with a smile on my face, eager to start the day.

At the end of the course I decided to stay on and join the community for a while. That weekend I took part in a Rebirthing course. The idea was to be conscious of our breathing and to take deep, continuous breaths. This was supposed to get us in touch with our childhood memories and even recreate our birth traumas. I didn't experience anything like that but I felt very peaceful with a deep sense of connection with the other participants. Part of the day was spent doing affirmations. The idea of creating your own reality had recently become very popular, mainly because of a bestselling book "You Can Heal Your Life" by Louise Hay. I got completely involved in this process.

One of my main affirmations was *I am finding the community of my dreams in an ideal location.* I would read it aloud to myself in the mirror. Then I would sing it. Then I would say it in the second person,

"You, Nigel are finding the community of your dreams..." and then in the third person, "Nigel is finding... etc."

And then I would sing it again and try to repeat it as often as possible each day. I kept this up for the three weeks that I stayed at Monkton Wyld. The community survived by running residential courses to supplement their income and I realised that this would be how my community would have to survive. There were very few places at that time offering residential courses and even fewer in sunny locations.

So off I went with my backpack, my guitar, my black hat and my stud in my left ear, heading for sunnier climes.

I headed south, down through France, still reciting my affirmation and quietly confident that something would turn up. I looked at several places along the way but it was only when I got to Andalucia in the south of Spain that I realised that this was where my community was meant to be. Andalucia at that time had a very slow pace of life and the people were relaxed and friendly. It reminded me a little bit of Ireland, except that here the sun shone brightly. Some places I rejected straight away. Mojacar in Almeria for example; too many drunks. Other parts of Almeria were too dry. Most of the coast of southern Spain was already built up, commercialised and expensive. I would have to search inland. I looked at a number of properties but still nothing was suitable. Spain had only recently recovered from almost forty years of dictatorship and there was a huge divide between the rich and the poor. Consequently as soon as I left the tourist spots on the coast, there were no suitable properties in the middle price bracket.

One fine day I arrived in the market town of Orgiva, just south of Granada. It wasn't a particularly attractive town. The older part of the town was quite charming in its own way but tacky, modern buildings were starting to rear their ugly heads in the newer parts. The setting though, was magnificent. I could see in the distance the snow covered tips of the Sierra Nevada mountain range and closer at hand a fertile valley dotted with ancient olive trees, some of them up to 2000 years old as well as a variety of citrus trees.

I walked into a local bar and announced to nobody in particular,

"Does anyone have a property for sale?"

There was an immediate reaction. It seemed that everyone in the bar had some sort of property to sell. One gentleman insisted that I come and see his fabulous property straight away. On the way out I met Carlos from Luxembourg. He told me in heavily accented Spanish that he had a property for sale but that nobody wanted to buy it and that anyway, he wasn't sure if he wanted to sell it to me. This "sales pitch" was intriguing because it was so unlike anything I had heard before. I asked if I could visit the property on my return and he was most insistent that if I were not back in fifteen minutes, he would be gone. The house I went to see was worse than I had imagined, just a few chicken sheds and a ramshackle house. I returned to the bar just in time to catch Carlos as he was making his exit.

We drove out of town on a rickety old dirt track, passing a smoking rubbish dump, altogether an inauspicious preparation for visiting a property. We turned up onto an even rougher dirt track and came to a large wall with a huge wooden door.

I walked through that door and I had what people call an epiphany moment. The property was called Cortijo Romero and it was beautiful, beyond my wildest dreams. I remember getting goose pimples and feeling like I had dropped a tab of acid. Everything seemed to be in technicolour. I'd been searching and visualising a property for two months and suddenly I'd found what I had been looking for. The buildings were in a state of disrepair. Carlos had lovingly constructed the property on top of what had been an old farmhouse. He was an antique dealer amongst other things and he bought old doors and windows and incorporated them into the buildings. It was built in the Moroccan style with a huge wall around it, with the inner part of the house within a walled courtyard. There were only two bedrooms but four new ones were under construction. There was a large dining room and sitting room which Carlos used as a restaurant. It was rarely open however, as guests had to book in advance and Carlos didn't have a telephone. There was a large garage which could be converted into three bedrooms. A lovely oval shaped swimming pool with a large crack down the middle was set in the middle of the garden. There were two rooms in the inner courtyard which could be converted into a large group room, once the leaky roof had been replaced. I envisaged stairs going up to a terrace on the roof above the group room. It had been landscaped in good taste with young palm trees dotted around the property.

Seeing that it would be a perfect place to build a community and to run courses I realised that it simply needed an investment of cash. The price was lower than I had expected as it had been on the market for a couple of years. It was nevertheless a lot more than I could afford but I was confident that I could raise the money. And so I told him that I was happy to pay the asking price. However, as I soon discovered, nothing was straight forward with Carlos. The next day he came up with a complicated story about why he needed another few thousand pesetas and I reluctantly agreed. We made a contract on the 31st December 1985, and I went back to the UK to send the money over to him. Not as easy as it sounds but I was on a mission. The force was with me! I really felt guided and unstoppable and I managed to raise the money, getting credit from banks in England, Scotland and Spain. I hated going into debt, not my style at all, but I could see clearly that there could be no half measures for this project if it were to work.

It was obvious to me what needed to be done on the property and I was extremely lucky to find a team of six young men, eager to get their hands on a big project. I gave them three months to finish the job and this included building ten new bedrooms with bathrooms.

Carlos was very helpful in the whole process of planning and decision making and the workers were brilliant. They worked hard and joyfully and with a very happy team spirit. At the same time I found a plumber, an electrician and a digger man with a machine to reshape the terraces in the garden. This was a huge job because the terraces were in a state of disrepair.

I then made a quick trip to England to hire group leaders to run the courses. My plan was to run a series of two week events, mostly on the theme of Rebirthing which I had found to be so life transforming. I threw in one or two 1 week courses at the end of the season in November on themes such as yoga and movement. I had read the publicity of a centre in Greece called Skyros where they run two week courses and where community spirit was emphasised. I decided that guests would be asked to take turns to help with the washing up to build a family atmosphere.

My next task was to make a brochure. I spent a lot of money which I didn't have on a glossy brochure. I knew from my study of marketing that it is vitally important to have faith in your project and invest a lot on advertising to initiate the project. The group leaders gave me their mailing lists, so that I could distribute my brochure widely.

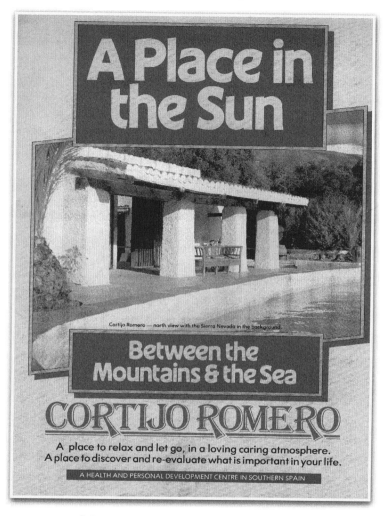

My first ever brochure for Cortijo Romero

I arranged to pay them according to how many people attended their courses, so they were strongly motivated to recruit students.

At the Rebirthing retreat at Monkton Wyld I had met some wonderful people and I was delighted when two of them, Marie and John, agreed to act as my booking agents in the UK. The building work went extremely well and was finished in April, right on time and we had a wonderful party to celebrate their excellent work.

Hugh, an excellent carpenter from Yorkshire made cupboards for all the bedrooms and kitchen and he and his wife Rita did the painting and decorating. I made a trip to Murcia in eastern Spain and I remember ordering 20 beds and a vast assortment of furniture. Rita was an experienced cook and I hired her to cook lunches and dinners.

Finally, Cortijo Romero was ready to open for business. It had been extremely hard work but it had all been done with a great deal of harmony and everyone involved was excited about the project.

TWELVE

LIFE AT CORTIJO ROMERO

The great day arrived, the opening day of Cortijo Romero on June 21st, 1986. The first course was to be a one week course led by Ray Brooks from the UK. The theme was Rebirthing, focused deep breathing to release childhood and birth traumas.

I had bought a small Renault 4 van, the type you have to pull the gear stick towards you to change gear. I had commissioned a lovely big round hand-woven carpet for the group room which seemed to be taking forever to be completed. It wasn't till the very day of opening that it was finally ready. Heaving a big sigh of relief, I picked it up from Granada that morning and then made my way to meet the first guests at Malaga airport.

Somehow all eight of us and our luggage managed to squeeze into that little car with the enormous carpet on the top. In those days the journey from Malaga to Cortijo Romero took three hours and it was very late by the time we got home. I was exhausted by then and was awoken next morning by a very polite woman.

"Excuse me, Nigel, but we were wondering if there was anything for breakfast?"

I'd been so busy with so many other things that I'd forgotten all about breakfast. Fortunately one of the guests who had arrived in her own car the previous evening had had time to forage in the kitchen and was able to make a reasonable breakfast. People were so in love with the beauty of the place and the excitement of a new venture that they were very forgiving.

We assembled later that morning, sitting in a circle in the group room on the new carpet. It was a wonderful moment. I've done it! I've done it! I kept saying to myself.

Rita arrived later to take care of lunch and dinner. I didn't have any other help those first weeks. Irene, who was to be my manager and helper was not due for another three weeks. I was able to join in with some of the sessions but not all of them because I had to do the shopping and make sure that everyone was comfortable.

The Rebirthing process brought up many emotions for my guests. There were tears and cries of anguish but also a lot of joy and celebration. People sat around the pool, mostly naked, singing and dancing. It was an altogether splendid week. It was followed by another two week long Rebirthing course which was led by Marie Frazer-Nash who was also my booking agent.

After Marie's course finished I was very relieved when Irene finally arrived. She was a lovely, smiling, young Irish woman and a delight to have around. Thank God, I thought. Great; she can do the shopping. And then I suddenly remembered that Irene couldn't drive and the shops were about a mile away. No problem; I took her for a little driving lesson and she even managed to more or less master the strange gear stick. I say more or less because I'd unfortunately forgotten to show her how to get into reverse and it took a couple of weeks for her to master that. Just as well there were not a lot of cars around in those days and she always managed to park without having to reverse.

Money was very tight around that time. I had negotiated loans in England and Spain, but my main source of income was my bank account in Scotland which I'd had for twenty years. I would get distraught letters from Mr. Morton, the bank manager informing me that I must reduce my borrowing. Mid-summer in Orgiva is a little bit hot for me, so leaving Irene in charge I went back to Scotland to see my family and to pay a visit to Mr. Morton, one of several visits. He was a golfer and we would always start with a long conversation about the ins and outs of golf. After about half an hour we'd get up to say goodbye and he would nonchalantly say,

"Nigel, you will eventually get that overdraft of yours down, won't you?"

I returned to Cortijo Romero. An old friend Rahmana that I'd met in India was now lending Irene a hand. Just as well. There had been a crisis. One of the guests had had a psychotic attack and had to be taken back to the UK. Unbeknown to us, he had been unstable for some months and the combination of the hot sun, the music, the intense therapy and the naked women by the pool sent him off the edge.

It was very hard work. One group of guests would leave on a Saturday morning, looking happy and enthusiastic. A cleaning team would arrive and then the new guests would come from the airport later in the day, looking grey and exhausted, needing a lot of comfort and care.

Picking up people at the airport was problematic. This was before mobile phones and I didn't have a landline either. It sounds incredible as I look back but I wanted a different approach to life. I thought if we didn't have phones, we would intuitively know when, say, to call by the plumber's house or meet the electrician in a cafe. And it worked surprisingly often. Finding drivers to pick up our guests without a telephone wasn't easy either but somehow we managed. To organise the airport trip, I would go to the local bar every Thursday night to phone Marie in England and she would tell me who was coming and on what flight. We tried to meet most flights to keep waiting time at the airport to a minimum. Without mobiles we would sometimes miss our guests and they would arrive a few hours later somewhat disgruntled, having paid a lot of money for a taxi.

I was very idealistic in those early days. I believed that coffee was an unnecessary stimulant, that for every high there would be a low and it was therefore banned for the first couple of years. Similarly, alcohol was not allowed. A strange situation arose. If you remember, I'd bought the property from Carlos. He then built another property on the land he owned next door. A young German friend of his, Josep opened a small bar and restaurant next door and often, towards the end of the week, all the guests would be next door and Irene and I would be on our own. Reluctantly I agreed to let our guests buy alcohol from the town and drink it on the premises.

Another thing that was very important for me was that once the guests arrived, I didn't want there to be any exchange of money. They paid for the holiday beforehand and once they were here they were my guests and wouldn't have to pay for anything. Many local artisans wanted to be able to sell their products at Cortijo Romero and I always resisted until one day, realising that I was swimming against the tide, allowed the sale of T-Shirts. They were made by Gel, the wife of Paul who has been the tour guide at Cortijo Romero for the last thirty years.

Similarly I didn't want my guests to be paying for massages. My idea was that there would be such a spirit of harmony that guests would spontaneously massage each other. The clientele of Cortijo Romero was far younger in those days, mostly people in their 30's and 40's. Surely they'd be able to exchange massages. Paying money for a massage seemed to me like another aspect of consumerism. It turned out that I was wrong. They didn't often take the time to massage each other and there was definitely a demand for external masseurs. Again I relented.

Irene, as well as being paid a pittance, was on a tight budget for buying food. I remember one guest, Ken asking for eggs for breakfast and when Irene explained that it was beyond her budget he forked out the money for the eggs. Irene was extremely hard working and loyal but there were times when we were both exhausted.

Luckily word of Cortijo Romero had started to spread and that first summer young travellers would arrive and, for board and keep were more than ready to lend a hand.

The food was vegetarian, not organic but it was locally produced. Intensive greenhouse farming which is now so prevalent in Andalucia had not yet started. Rita was a very good cook and I was fond of her even though she could be stubborn and would always speak her mind.

There was occasionally conflict which is bound to happen when people work hard for little remuneration. We would always try to resolve problems with group discussions and reach some kind of consensus. I was in a strange position. I believed in equality and that everyone should freely speak their minds. And yet it was me that was worrying about the fact that the business was losing money and it seemed to me that someone had to lay down the law occasionally.

Running a business was a new experience for me. When someone asked me once for a job description, it seemed like a foreign concept to me. Workers would be given a few guidelines and then would do what they felt needed to be done. Mostly this worked out fine. I wasn't very good at keeping accounts. Good management requires clarity and systems that work, that can be adapted so that people can readily understand what they have to do. This I was never good at.

What I did do well though, was to look after the guests. I would make sure to connect with them as soon as they arrived and try to make them feel comfortable and at ease. I would sing and create a party atmosphere at night, especially at the beginning of the week.

Some weeks I would tell the guests that a Spanish professor from Granada, an old friend of mine called Don Miguel would be coming to give a Spanish lesson and would be singing a few songs and playing the guitar. I made a bit of a song and dance about how the women should cover up their arms and legs because Spanish men can get a bit frisky as they are not used to seeing naked flesh. This was rather shaky ground because feminism was rife at the time. Most people however were curious and they expected that any flirting would be innocent, especially as Don Miguel had a wife and seven children.

I would have the guests assembled by the fire. The lights were turned off and candles were lit. Then I would quickly disguise myself as Don Miguel with a wig, dark glasses and a dark suit. Nobody had ever seen me formally dressed.

Don Miguel

I would knock on the door, a loud knock, and one of my helpers would open the door. "Hola, Don Miguel," she would exclaim and then I was off. I would flirt outrageously with men and women alike and sing well known songs such as La Bamba, Guantanamera and Cielito Lindo and I'd make up tunes so that they would know how to order drinks in the bar. My favourite was called "Jugo de Naranja" (orange juice). After a little while I would hear people nudge each other and whisper to their neighbor, "It's Nigel," and the whisper would go around the room.

One evening a good friend of mine who was a volunteer, Christine McKenna played the part of the angry wife of Don Miguel, bursting into the room. Christine had been a well known actress in the 70's starring in the TV series "The Flambards." She was a fearsome wife as she castigated Don Miguel for not looking after his seven children and I exited the room with my tail between my legs, much to the delight of our guests. A psychologist would probably say that there was some part of me that would have liked to behave in this way. There might well be something in it. As I grew older I went completely off the idea of playing the role of Don Miguel.

Somehow I found time to participate in the group therapy sessions. They were always interesting and it helped with the cohesion of the group if I were present. Most of the group leaders were more than happy to have me there. I started to learn the dynamics of group therapy. It seemed to me to be mostly about listening intently, being present and intuitive and occasionally saying a few words. One course had only five or six participants and the group leader, a Maltese man named Manas Marmara canceled. He felt drawn to go and work with the Hopi Indians. There were no contracts in those days. It was a little inconsiderate as I didn't get a great deal of notice but I could understand him. I think there was less sense of responsibility then. People just followed their intuition and their dreams. There was no time to find anyone else so I ran the group myself; the first of many. Thank you, Manas. You did me a big favour.

In those first groups that I ran, I didn't say all that much. I listened and let things happen. It was scary and sometimes it seemed like things would get out of control but it invariably worked out.

I remember one eminent psychologist, Glynn Seaborn Jones saying to me,

"Nigel, that's an interesting approach you have. Rogerian, isn't it?"

"Yes, that's right," I replied.

I hadn't the slightest idea what he was talking about but heck, my middle name was Rodger after all!

I was good at organising a structure for the group. As a community, we needed a framework that we could all work with. Mealtimes were sacred: 9 a.m. breakfast, 1.30 p.m. lunch and 7.30 p.m. dinner. We, the hosts would always eat with the guests, trying to ensure that we didn't all sit at the same table. Tuesday was the excursion day. I would hire drivers and we would go off for the day to explore the exquisite villages dotted around the foothills of the Sierra Nevada. Thursday mornings were an opportunity to visit the market in the local town of Orgiva.

It's interesting to note that thirty-five years later the new owner Alan Dale uses exactly this same time table and it's the same one that I use in my current centre in south west France, La Roane.

On reflection I probably spent too much time with the guests and not enough on staff and general administration. However our biggest problem was that the model we had chosen simply could not work in the long term. People came every single week and we didn't get a break. Certainly every worker or volunteer had a day off but I couldn't afford more than that. I was asking my staff to get involved with the guests in an intimate way but this is impossible to do week in and week out, no matter how wonderful the guests. We needed more time to ourselves.

I have fond and happy memories of the people who worked at Cortijo Romero. There was Ramon. He came to work for me as a gardener and odd job man in my second year of operation. He had been recently married and he was very interested in plants. I knew that he understood the complicated watering system that we used.

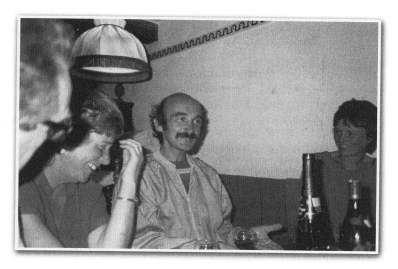

At Cortijo Romero

The whole of the region which is known as the Alpujarras is in the foothills of the Sierra Nevada mountain range just south of Granada. Hundreds of years ago the Moors built complicated irrigation systems, utilising the melting snows in the mountains to irrigate the whole valley through a series of channels called *aceicias*.

When I bought Cortijo Romero, included in the deeds was the right to use the water channel for half an hour each week. The problem was that the timing of the half hour changed weekly over a nine week cycle. It all seemed very complicated and I was delighted when Ramon took charge of it. He wasn't highly educated but he was intelligent, intuitive and hard working, except when he wasn't! He had a rhythm of his own and it took me some time to get used to it. Often I would see him sitting in a bar in town when he was supposed to be working. He always had a good excuse but nevertheless once a month we would have a show down and hard words would be said. In spite of this there was great mutual love and respect. He made the garden beautiful and I knew I could rely on him. He was my first point of contact with the local town, Orgiva, and he was always loyal and spoke highly of me.

His wife Graciela was the head cleaner. Every Saturday once the guests had left, all of Ramon's extended family would descend on Cortijo Romero to clean the place. The noise level was horrendous. They would shout and yell. It reminded me of my uncles and aunts playing bridge in the 1950's. But the work got done and I was very fond of them.

One aspect of the job that I really enjoyed was my contact with the group facilitators. They were often leaders in a field but were prepared to work for what was not a huge amount of money to support the project. Some of them, like Leo Rutherford, refused to take money for their services when they weren't many guests on the course. I had a huge respect for him. He was on a shamanic path and a lot of his work involved drumming and chanting. Now, Leo is not a singer and I feel that it takes courage and integrity to sing in public and get others to sing when it's not your strong point.

Some like Serge Beddington-Behrens, another wonderful group leader, would insist that the staff get involved in the therapeutic process. Indeed, we all did get involved that fortnight. A very strange thing happened on our excursion day. We all went down to a mountain stream for a picnic. After eating, a group of us, mostly men, went up to a waterfall and stood naked as the water cascaded over us. In our company was a young woman with large breasts which we guys couldn't stop ogling at, no matter how hard we tried to be discrete. We dressed and everyone left and went up to the bar in the nearby village.

I stayed a while, lying naked in the sun. Suddenly I was awoken from my revere by a bee stinging me on the penis. It was just a little prick but enough to make me shout out in alarm. I got dressed and joined the others. The first thing they said was,

"Don't tell me you got stung on the penis as well."

"But how did you know?" I asked in wonderment.

It turned out that two of the guys who had been down there had also been stung on the penis. It seemed that the bees were trying to tell us something but at that point in my life I was not yet ready to listen. Many beautiful women came to do the courses and as the owner, singer and entertainer, there were many women who were seduced by my charms. You have to remember that in the 80's boundaries between clients and therapists of any nature were less clear cut than nowadays. There was a spirit of anything goes. Most people swam naked in the pool and many new relationships blossomed in the hot Spanish sun.

Some aspects of the job I found very difficult. Spain had recently become part of the European Union and the local bureaucrats started poking their noses into my affairs. Health and Safety people in particular started to bother me. Our beautiful new wooden shelves in the kitchen so lovingly built by Hugh for example had to be replaced and made with stainless steel. They started to take more interest in my tax position. I earned my money in the UK and I had to start declaring more each year to the Spanish authorities to justify my expenditure.

When I bought Cortijo Romero there were very few neighbours but Carlos who owned the surrounding land started selling off building plots so that eventually there were houses dotted all over the neighbourhood. I could have easily bought this land cheaply but I was up to my neck in debt and it proved impossible at the time to borrow more. Money was always an issue for me at Cortijo Romero, especially in the beginning. I was trying to invoke principles of love and harmony but it becomes difficult when you don't have enough money to pay people a decent wage. Things gradually improved however as the years passed. My first year of business, I had an average of about six guests on each course. Sometimes they would only be three people on the course, but I would run it anyway. I hated having to cancel courses. I thought it was sending out a bad message to the universe. That year I made a loss and my overdraft was growing.

The second year I did a lot better. Word was spreading about Cortijo Romero. I invited journalists to stay free of charge and they would write favourable articles about their experience. More and more people were searching for answers to the stresses of modern life and were looking for something different. The second year I averaged twelve guests per course. This was about breakeven point, but I'd bought a second car to transport the guests and built another bedroom and my overdraft grew. I was getting desperate. I didn't know how long Mr. Morton, the bank manager, would support my spending.

Interest rates at the time were around 16 % and I was spending a lot of money simply repaying the interest. I then did something that I found extremely difficult. I went cap in hand to everyone I knew, relatives and friends, and asked them to lend me money at bank rate, which was considerably lower than I was paying on my overdraft. Thanks to all the generous help I received, I paid off my overdraft, much to the delight of Mr. Morton. With secure funding a lot of the strain was taken off my shoulders. I was determined to survive.

The third year I did really well. The average group size was fourteen which was excellent since we could only take a maximum of eighteen. Once I had passed the breakeven point and covered all my fixed costs (local rates, taxes, wages etc.) all the extra money was profit. I was making good money and that year I was able to pay off a lot of the loans I'd been given. The following year was even better and by the end of 1989, I had paid off virtually all my debts.

Sadly my wonderful manager Irene left at the end of my third year 1988. Irene had fought tooth and nail to support me and Cortijo Romero, but she'd had enough. She went on to have a successful career as a journalist in Cork, Ireland.

She was replaced in 1989 by the equally wonderful Maggie Whiteley who usually went by the name of Star. She was incredibly clear and insightful and I always got the impression that she got her ideas and her clarity from another dimension. By 1990, Cortijo Romero was functioning well. Star was doing a great job managing the place, and I no longer had so many financial worries.

However, I was suffering from burnout after five years of intense work getting the project off the ground, and I'd had enough. I was ready for a change. To my intense relief, Star and her friend Wendy agreed to rent Cortijo Romero from me and continue it as a going concern.

I have fond memories of my last course just before leaving. The group leader Julie Felix had been a well known folk singer in the 60's with her own TV series. She was the British equivalent of Joan Baez. Knowing that this was to be my last course I felt revitalised and ready to party. I'd invited various friends who'd been helpful over the years to come and join us.

Julie is a wonderful singer with a warm personality. Of Mexican origin, she sang in Spanish in the local bar, much to the delight of the locals. The day of Don Miguel's performance we took the vans and eventually walked up a rocky river bed to a cave where Don Miguel was to meet up with us. I managed to change into my Don Miguel guise without anyone seeing me and was able to make my usual grand entrance. The acoustics were fantastic and it was probably my best ever Don Miguel performance. By the time we were ready to come home it was almost dark. One of the women grumbled a little bit because she was in high heels. In my excitement I'd forgotten to tell her where we were going but we all managed to scramble home safely.

It had been a great week and I was sad to say goodbye to so many wonderful people. However I was hugely relieved to no longer have such immense responsibilities. The day after the course finished I left Cortijo Romero and flew off to the UK for the next stage of my life.

THIRTEEN

RACHEL

It was just before leaving Cortijo Romero that I first met Rachel. She was 28, from the UK, and I liked her from the very first moment we met at the airport when she arrived to do a one week course. She was highly attractive, intelligent, she smiled a lot and yes, she laughed at my jokes! What more could you want? I was involved with other women at the time. After Rachel's first visit we agreed to meet up in a fortnight. She was living in Barcelona and the rendezvous point was Alicante which was situated halfway between us. I almost pulled out. Star had been giving me a hard time about my womanizing activities, saying it wasn't correct behavior and I was almost convinced that she was right, but then I thought, no. I like her. It would be a pity not to take it further. We had even discussed on our first night together whether things might work out between us as a long term couple. The weekend in Alicante went really well. We swam, we lay under a blanket on the beach and kissed in secret and we made love on a very creaky bed.

Later that month we spent a week in the seaside resort of Nerja and after that we decided to live together in the UK. We ended up living very near to the mystical town of Glastonbury in Somerset, in a big manor house which we called the "Manna House". We lived as a community of spiritual seekers and it was mostly very harmonious.

One day Rachel announced that she was pregnant. How to deal with this situation? We decided to get married and told Rachel's parents. I had met them previously; lovely people but conservative and middle class. Rachel's mother, Brenda's first words on hearing the news were,

"Nigel, you're going to have to get yourself a suit for the wedding."

They were a bit concerned that I was fifteen years older than Rachel. Nevertheless, they turned out to be tolerant of what was for them my unusual behaviour. They got used to my standing on my head in the garden, my guitar playing and my strict vegetarianism. At dinner Rachel's dad Roger, would sometimes bring up the subject of "homos" (homosexuals) and there would be animated discussions about the rights and wrongs of it. Bless him; he was amazingly open for someone who had been to public school, Oxford and served in the British Army.

*Above: At the Registry Office signing marriage papers
after my fit of giggles*

*Below: Wedding photo with three elder brothers,
two sisters-in-law, father-in-law and two nieces*

By the time of the wedding, Rachel was already six months pregnant. Her belly was swelling and the dressmaker had to let out her dress from time to time. The legal ceremony was done in a registry office. I had to say, "I, Nigel, solemnly declare," but the words wouldn't come out. I started to laugh hysterically and I couldn't stop. I looked around and saw my three elder brothers grinning sheepishly. Rachel's mother Brenda seemed less amused. Again and again I started, "I solemnly declare...," and then more giggles and laughter.

"Don't worry," said the Registrar, trying to calm me down. "Take your time. We've got another fifteen minutes before the next wedding."

"Get on with it, Nigel!" barked Brenda. I was so surprised that I managed to get it all out as required, all in one breath. We were married. I kissed the bride and everyone heaved a sigh of relief.

We held the civil ceremony in a stately home. Star from Cortijo Romero acted as the vicar. Rachel's friends and family were on the right side of the aisle and my friends and family were on the left. Star opened the ceremony.

"We've all been waiting for this marriage for a long time; those of you on the left for longer than those of you on the right." It was a nice way to break the ice. We made vows and threw objects symbolically representing our past lives into a large fire that had been set up for the purpose. I was in tears by then. Our musician friends from the Manna House sang beautifully. It was altogether a wonderful wedding.

A few months later our baby was due to be born. We had opted for a home birth. When Rachel's contractions started, all of us at the Manna House gathered around her bedside to offer our prayers and support. Jenny, one of the residents of the Manna House, had been studying acupuncture and she stuck needles in Rachel to try to speed up the process. However, our baby didn't seem keen to show up and after many hours of labour we were taken in an ambulance with a blazing siren to the nearest hospital. We went full speed over a humpback bridge, expressly to try to encourage the baby to come; all to no avail. We arrived in the hospital, the staff looking warily at the acupuncture needles sticking out of Rachel's face. Hours later after a great deal of agony, a baby boy was born. He had the umbilical cord round his neck and looked a funny shade of blue. He was immediately put in an incubator. He was over ten pounds in weight. He looked like a giant in comparison with the others in special care who had all been born prematurely.

He emerged five days later from the incubator and I remember carrying him through the hospital with great satisfaction. An elderly woman approached me.

"Proud grandfather, eh?" she said conversationally. Do I look that old I thought to myself? I'm only 44.

"No, I'm the father actually," I replied.

"Second time around, eh?" she offered. I wished she'd shut up.

"No, it's my first marriage."

"Well, better late than never," she said cheerily. Fuck off! I was thinking to myself, but this being England, I smiled sweetly and said nothing.

We called him Leo after a character in a book called "Journey to the East" by one of my favourite authors Herman Hesse and also because that was his astrological sign.

Rachel and I had read a book called "The Continuum Concept" about an anthropologist who goes to the Amazon and concludes that parents should sleep with their baby lying between them. Readers, I can vouchsafe that this is very bad for your sex life and what's more, you are not likely to get a lot of sleep. Babies burp, pass wind and sniffle all night long and roll all over the bed.

In addition Leo had an awful affliction called colic for the first four months of his life and he cried a lot. When he started, I would discretely take myself off to another room.

He had great difficulty getting to sleep. I used to take him for long walks and as he sat on my backpack he would gradually fall asleep.

Another favourite technique was to take him for a drive and when the music for the radio series "The Archers" came on he would fall asleep straight away.

I needed to find a job as the rent from Cortijo Romero wasn't enough to support us and we decided that it would be a good idea for me to train to be a teacher. We moved to South Wales for me to do a one year course teachers' training course. I got excellent grades for my teaching skills although the teachers did not always know what to make of me. I remember one teaching assignment where we had to imagine that our class mates were young eight year old students and we were asked to talk to them about going on vacation. I got the class to shut their eyes and I talked them through a creative visualisation where they went to the airport, got in the plane and arrived in hot, sunny Spain. They got taken to a lovely hotel with a swimming pool and there, sitting in a hammock was a wonderful Spanish singer to serenade them.

By then I had undressed and was in my bathing trunks with sunglasses and I proceeded to play my guitar and sing La Bamba. The other students laughed uproariously but the teacher in charge found it highly embarrassing. I was a lot older than her and she wasn't sure whether to laugh or to tell me off. In the end she did neither.

It wasn't easy to find work at that time as there was a lot of unemployment in the UK but after completing my training I got offered a job in a small school in Liverpool. It was a charity school for disaffected teenagers who didn't thrive in the normal school system. There were only ten kids in the school and we were two teachers, Francis and I. Rachel and I decided to job-share. She had trained as a teacher and she worked one and a half days while I worked the rest of the week, taking it in turns to look after Leo.

We found Liverpool to be very strange. People were extremely friendly but there seemed to be an ingrained culture of theft. The kids in our school unanimously considered for example, that it was perfectly okay to steal a bicycle if you were late going home and might get into trouble with your parents. "Well, it's their fault for not locking it up," they would claim defensively. We would often be offered machine tools or musical equipment at run down prices for what obviously were stolen goods.

Teaching in Wales

Rachel found central Liverpool too crowded, not an ideal environment for bringing up a child and we settled in the seaside resort of Formby, just north of Liverpool. This was an extremely conservative town. Twice I almost got arrested. Once when I was with my son Leo on the beach, a policeman approached us and started asking me lots of questions. After about ten minutes he apologised,

"Sorry Sir, I thought you were a hippie". And so? I was tempted to say but didn't. Not clever to mess around with policemen in Formby. On another occasion I was standing on the garden wall of our home, playing with

Leo, when two police cars screeched to a halt outside our house. The police informed Rachel that there was a suspicious looking individual in the garden.

"Ah, that will be my husband," she replied.

One of the best things that came from our stay in Formby, was the birth of our daughter Anna. We insisted on a home birth, much to the annoyance of our doctor who refused us any further treatment. Anna was born in a hot tub without any complications. Two days after she was born, she looked up at me and smiled broadly. I felt a warm glow in my heart and a sense of deja vu.

One year of teaching was enough for us and we decided to go back to Spain. Star was struggling with Cortijo Romero and I felt that it was time to put it up for sale. Within a month of putting it on the market I had a buyer, Alan Dale. Alan was the perfect buyer. He didn't want to make any big changes. He kept more or less the same staff, the same time table and the same vegetarian cuisine. He ran the outfit from the UK with his son Ali in charge of things in Spain. To this day Alan has continued running Cortijo Romero and many thousands of people have had life changing experiences there. I have been going there every year since 1993, to run one week courses, based on the themes of music, yoga and having fun. I still love the place and get treated like royalty. I particularly love to see Ramon, the gardener and Graciela the head cleaner who I first employed thirty-three years ago when they were in their 20's.

Orgiva, the local town has changed quite dramatically since I went there in the 80's. When I first arrived in Orgiva there were almost no foreigners staying there. However, a neighbour, Chris Stewart published a best-selling book about settling in the area "Driving over Lemons." That, and subsequent books that he wrote encouraged many people from all over Europe who were looking for an alternative sort of lifestyle, to come and settle in the area. In addition many guests of Cortijo Romero were so enthralled by the region that they decided to come and try to make a new life for themselves. Nowadays I think of it as some sort of Wild West version of Glastonbury or Sedona with all its mystics, yogis and hippies.

After selling Cortijo Romero, I was now rich. It was time to buy another property. Rachel had very clear ideas about the sort of property she wanted. It included a stream or river running through it and it had to be donkey riding distance from the nearest village. We had a vague idea to set up some sort of spiritual community based on permaculture. I say vague because I didn't have a lot of enthusiasm or clarity about undertaking another big project as Cortijo Romero had been such a huge effort.

I went along with Rachel. She was fifteen years younger than me and had never done a big project and I didn't want to disappoint her. Spain is a very dry country and such properties are very difficult to find. We settled in the area just north of Gibraltar, near a town called Gaucin where I set about looking for a property to buy.

I remember one night when I was having difficulty sleeping with two children in the room and so I moved to the room next door. As I was trying to get to sleep, I started to have a strong feeling that Sally who had been the family nanny for forty years and who had died a couple of years previously, was present in the room.

Anna, who was now about a year old, had been conceived about a year after Sally's death. By a strange coincidence, the room in which she was conceived was the same room where Sally had some sixty years previously slept, when she worked as a maid for the former owner, a retired army colonel. As I lay on my bed trying to sleep, I could hear or I thought I could hear the sounds of the Scottish music that Sally loved so well.

"Sally," I said, half aloud, half to myself, "I know you're there. Can you give me a sign?"

Just at that precise moment Anna woke up and started to cry. I had goose pimples on my skin. Anna was a good sleeper.

Sally with Leo shortly before her death

It was only 1 a.m. and she never usually woke up at that time of the night. My first thought was that Sally had reincarnated as Anna. I don't know if it's true or not but it's a nice idea.

We moved from house to house but as the search continued, we both grew increasingly frustrated. Eventually we consulted a clairvoyant who advised us to go to France because our son Leo had some sort of connection with France and would be much happier there. It seemed like a reasonable idea. Why not? In my search I was just trying to be open to guidance as to where to settle. I had decided not to try the creative visualisation that I had used to find Cortijo Romero.

I was content to go with the flow and to look for clues and see where we ended up.

Leaving Rachel to look after Leo, I headed off to France via the town of Nerja where I was to spend the weekend attending a sound healing course. On the last day of the course I mislaid my car keys on a pebbled beach and although I spent over an hour looking for them, they were nowhere to be found. I knew it would take another week or two to have a replacement key sent to me but, undeterred I finished the course and slept soundly that night. Next morning I got up, went to the beach and walked straight to the keys. For me at that time it was a symbolic find, as if I were being given the keys for my new home. I made my way to France. I had a reasonable understanding of French from school, enough to make myself understood and so I was able to talk to estate agents.

My friend Melanie had recommended an estate agent called Marion in Villfranche-sur-Rourergue, an hour north of Toulouse and she proved to be a gem. She was a large woman, married to a man a good twenty-five years her junior. She was a *bon vivant*, fond of wine, cigarettes and sausages and passionate about jazz. She would never show me the upstairs of houses and it soon dawned on me that with the weight she was carrying around, it wasn't easy for her to get up the stairs. I liked her and most of all I trusted her, always an issue when you arrive in a new country and don't know anyone.

There were plenty of properties available. Since the French Revolution, France unlike Spain had had a big middle class, many of whom had built quite substantial properties. In recent years many of the middle classes had left the countryside and drifted into the cities, leaving a lot of vacant houses. This was before the invasion of foreigners buying up properties which happened quite soon after our arrival. I was in a buyers' market.

After I had been in France for about a week, Marion showed me a property near the historic town of St Antonin-Noble-Val. The main house was habitable with four bedrooms and there was an old farmhouse built in the 1840's where the original subsistence farmers had lived until the 1960's, plus an old barn from the same period. The buildings were set in a twenty acre estate, half forest and half pasture. It was raining heavily when I first saw it, not an auspicious beginning. The owners Monsieur and Madame Fabry were an unusual couple. Monsieur had been a prisoner of the Germans during the war and was now a retired vet who looked after his sheep grazing in the garden. It was his way of keeping the vast lawn cut. He was a big, hefty man and proud of it. Every time I saw him he would tell me how he once carried a piano on his back up the stairs, single handed. Madame was some twenty-five years younger than Monsieur and she was obsessively tidy. She went berserk when I, trying to get out of the pouring rain, entered the house for the first time without wiping my feet properly and muddied her tiles.

It was the first property that had seemed at all suitable so I made them an offer. I explained to Rachel who was still in Spain, that there was no river or stream running through it and that it was three miles from the nearest village but by then she was so fed up with being unsettled that she was prepared to go along with whatever I came up with. My offer was accepted and I drove fifteen hours from Spain through the night with Rachel, two very young children and all our possessions. Every time I ever saw Monsieur Fabry in subsequent months there would be first the piano story and then his regrets that he had sold the property so cheaply to me. It's true that when many foreigners started settling in the area in the following years, he would have gotten a lot more for it had he waited.

Living in France took some getting used to. We lived in an isolated area and often craved company. Our limited knowledge of French didn't help.

View of our local village St. Antonin

Also, the French seemed much more formal than their Spanish neighbours. Tradesmen would come to the door and we would offer them coffee.

"*Non, c'est ne pas l'heure.* No, it's not the proper time," they would reply.

Coffee was taken early in the morning with a croissant and again straight after lunch. Lunch was eaten at 12 o'clock. At 11.45 they would be saying *bon appetit* to us as they were about to eat their midday meal. It seems strange to us because we'd not long finished breakfast. Lunch was a long drawn out affair, often lasting two hours with intense conversation. What did they find to talk about? I soon realised that the main topic of conversation was food. They would go into great detail about the merits of different types of gourmet food. This was the land of the infamous *foie gras,* the liver of ducks who had been force fed. My vegetarian diet was little understood. For my fist meal in a restaurant, when I told the waitress that my vegetable soup had bits of meat in it she replied,

"Ca c'est rien, c'est seulement des lardons. Oh, that's nothing, just tiny bits of ham."

It was difficult making friends with our limited French. We found few kindred spirits. The bar would at first go quiet when I walked in with my bright coloured clothes and sombrero but I quickly got into the local habit of announcing a general *bonjour* to the assembled company and that seemed to help. When you have poor command of the language though, it's easy to lose confidence in yourself. You feel you have little to offer to people. It is difficult to crack spontaneous jokes and make small talk in the supermarket for example, but I took lessons and persevered.

Sometimes there were a few quite embarrassing misunderstandings. On one occasion I took a package containing my faeces to the post office to send to

Germany for analysis because I suspected that I had candida. I quickly looked up the word for faeces *"selle"* but I found out later that it also mean salt or a saddle. After queueing for a while I finally got to the counter and told the lady in my best French,

"I want to send a package to Germany," She was very businesslike.

"What's in it?" she asked.

" *Ma selle*," I replied.

"Salt?" she asked, looking mystified. "It's certainly not a saddle."

"No," I replied, highly embarrassed. "It's er em....caca," I whispered.

The queue behind me seemed to be getting bigger by the minute and they were all listening intently. *"Ah, les selles!"* she replied in a loud voice, glad to have solved the mystery. *"D'un animal?* From an animal?" she enquired innocently.

"No, it's em..er.. mine." By now I could hear tittering in the background.

"And you want to send it all the way to Germany?" she asked incredulously.

"Yes," I replied meekly.

"Well, this is all highly irregular. I will have to speak to the manager."

The post office was now full and everyone was enjoying the spectacle. The manager arrived and the same questions were asked with the same answers and the same tittering in hushed tones behind me. That yes, I did indeed want to send my poo all the way to Germany. Obviously by the reaction in the room, this had never been done before in the long history of France. Finally, the package was dispatched and I left the post office, trying desperately to avoid eye contact with any of the other customers.

Our local town of St Anonin is stunningly beautiful. It was founded in the sixth century and by the Middle Ages was a flourishing town, specializing in tanning hides and pressing walnuts to extract the oil. It was a hub of commerce via the River Aveyron which borders the town and which eventually makes its way to Bordeaux on the Atlantic. Parts of the town resemble a rabbit warren and after twenty-five years I'm still discovering new streets. It boasts the oldest civic building in France, the town hall, now a museum which was built in the 12th century. Another interesting feature is the *La Maison d'Amour*, the former bath house which was rumored to have been a brothel. The door is adorned with an ancient sculpture of a kissing couple.

In recent years the town has been the backdrop for two Hollywood films. The first one was "Charlotte Grey" with Cate Blanchett based on a book by Sebastian Faulks. It was a fictional account of the German occupation during the war. I was lucky enough to get the part of an extra and my role was to sit in a bar, smoking Gitanes whilst Cate had dealings with a fellow spy. It was fascinating to watch the film being produced. The central part of the village had been completely revamped to resemble the 1940's. Houses were painted with special paint which peeled instantly to give them an authentic look. I was playing my role alongside some old men who had been in the French resistance. The war had been very hard on them as the film shows and the wounds had not yet healed. The local hairdresser, Philipe played the part of a Nazi officer and some of these old-timers were so disgusted that they subsequently refused to continue coming to his salon.

The second film "The Hundred Foot Journey" starring Helen Mirren, was an altogether lighter theme about the competition between a *cordon bleu* restaurant and an upstart Indian restaurant, and the eventual love stories involving the two sides.

Little by little we started to feel more settled. There were so many ways to entertain ourselves. We made canoe trips down the river Aveyron with stunningly beautiful cliffs in the background. There were many caves in these cliffs to explore, where the resistance fighters had hidden during the war. Some dear friends from the UK, Rana and Melanie, had settled in the area and we started to make good friends with French people. Many of them had come from other parts of France, attracted by the beauty of St Antonin. The children were growing up and were very soon bilingual. Our son Leo who had had a difficult start did indeed take to life in France, just as the clairvoyant in Spain had foretold. His first few days at school though were traumatic as his teacher was a bit of a dragon. However, the teacher from the class above, Claudine, was a sweetheart and she took him under her wing. For three months he said not a word. One day he suddenly started to speak with the perfect local twang. Claudine later told us that it had brought tears of relief to her eyes.

I gave some yoga classes and Rachel started to do the same. She also started to teach English. Rachel and I almost never spent quality time together and were often too tired by the time the children had gone to bed. We rarely went out together as she was never too keen on leaving the children with babysitters. I wouldn't say that we were ecstatically happy but the children were doing well and we seemed to be settling down to life in France.

FOURTEEN

DIVORCE

As the years passed it turned out that life as a nuclear family, living in an isolated farm, away from friends and family wasn't easy. Rachel was a creative and dedicated mother, so good in fact that I often felt inadequate. I didn't have a clear direction in my life. We were surviving financially by renting out our homes in the summer whilst living temporarily in a yurt, but I was lacking the company of inspiring friends. Rachel's first priority was the two children. That seemed fine to me but I sometimes felt that she seemed to care more about our ducks, chickens and cats than she did about me.

She was still very dependent on me as my French was a lot better than hers and I was therefore the main point of contact with the outside world. I seemed to be just drifting along without any clear idea of where I was going and Rachel was growing restless. I was nevertheless very secure in the relationship. Divorce was unheard of in our family or indeed in Scotland when I was growing up. Even when Rachel confided to me that she had had a crush on a visitor passing through our lives, alarm bells never rang in my head. I thought I must just accept this as a passing whim rather than really look at any problems we might have.

I signed up to do a voice therapy workshop in the UK. Rachel was supportive. She was keen for me to have inspiration and direction in my life. The course lasted five days and I spoke to her occasionally on the phone. After the course ended I went to Bournemouth to stay with Marie and John, my former booking agents at Cortijo Romero. On the Saturday night I had a strong feeling that there was something wrong in our marriage. It was as if the energy lines which existed between our two beings had been suddenly ruptured. I came home. She met me at the airport and we both pretended that nothing was wrong. I was sure it would all work out, like it always did whenever we had had a row. We arrived home. She was hosting a shiatsu course which was taking place in another house on the property. There was a mutual friend, Jean-Louis taking part in the course and I suspected that she was fond of him.

I asked her, "Is there anything going on between you and Jean-Louis?" I fully expected her to say that she quite liked him, but that it was just a passing fantasy. And there and then, February 23, 1999 she told me that she had fallen in love with him and wanted to leave me. I couldn't believe it and yet, she was adamant.

"Hit me!" she said, "I deserve it."

It was nothing, if not dramatic. No thanks, I thought to myself. It wasn't really my style even though I was furious. Then she offered her body, thinking that if we made love we might rekindle some magic; to no avail. She was still very clear about leaving me the next day.

"Is this the end of the road?" I asked.

"Yes, I'm afraid so," she replied again and again with great finality.

I was distraught. I felt empathy with Jesus on the cross when he said, "My God why have you forsaken me?" I am not exaggerating. I realised that I had always felt protected. I had done some pretty crazy things in my life but it had always turned out more or less okay.

I couldn't accept it. I thought there must be a mistake, that I'd wake up and it was all a bit of a misunderstanding. My anger was against Jean-Louis, my former friend. I went to my punch-bag and imagined I was punching him in the face. Two days later he suffered a blow doing Aikido and nearly lost an eye. Coincidence? Possibly, but it sent shivers down my spine. I realised that I must not direct my anger at him. Even in my distressed state I knew that when we direct violence at others it has a habit of coming back to us tenfold in some guise or other.

And yet I wasn't always able to think so clearly. One morning a well meaning friend told me that Jean-Louis had been trying to seduce my wife for months. So incensed was I that I remember walking around the town, where I knew he was out shopping, hoping to meet him and punch him in the face. Nights I spent walking round and round the kitchen table.

"Keep moving," I said to myself. "Don't give in." Round and round I went, sometimes until three in the morning.

My mother was always a great help around this time. She would always counsel me never to quarrel with Rachel and to always think of the children first. Easier said than done, but I think that on the whole I managed to succeed. I remember fondly my cousins Terry and Gerald who told me that I must phone them at any time of the day or night whenever I felt that I needed a shoulder to cry on.

By now Rachel had moved into a house with a friend and a few weeks later she moved in with Jean-Louis. She looked after the children who were five and seven at the time four days a week and I had them for three days. Leo was less affected by the separation. Anna found it more difficult.

Above: Leo aged 14 runs faster than me. Our last ever race.

Below: With Leo, 2015

Many years later Anna confided to me that she had tried to sabotage her mother's new relationship by stuffing toilet paper down the toilet to try to alienate Jean-Luis from the family. However, in time she also got used to the new situation.

It was a full time job being miserable. I grew forgetful. I would thoughtlessly leave valuables in public places. If anyone were to even suggest that Jean-Louis was an attractive man and they could understand Rachel, I would be furious. I thought I would drown the pain and somehow get revenge by finding another girlfriend but I was too toxic and bitter, not considered attractive qualities by members of the opposite sex.

I have only one happy memory in all that time. I went to the Skyros Centre in Greece for a holiday and I remember sitting in the terrace of a bar, talking to a woman and for the whole afternoon that we chatted, I never thought once of Rachel.

It took almost a year before I had another girlfriend. This was Celine, a lovely young French artist who would talk non-stop. I loved to listen to her and my French improved rapidly but I was not in love with her and after nine months we parted.

The hardest thing for me in those years was seeing Jean-Louis with my kids. Our local town is quite small and everyone knew our business. Fortunately nobody took sides. My anger was directed towards Jean-Louis. This was quite irrational. It takes two to tango but this was pure jealousy and insecurity that was motivating me.

It's such a cliché, but time, as you all know, is indeed a great healer. I didn't want to remain an angry victim all my life. Things gradually improved. Three or four years after our separation, Rachel suggested that Jean-Louis and I act in a play together. This was a big challenge, but I felt that it would help me to move on with my life and perhaps even rekindle some sort of friendship with Jean-Louis. The plan was to do a play in English and in French about an English couple (myself and a wonderful English actress called Mandy) and a French couple (Jean-Louis and Catherine, a lovely, bubbly French girl with a great voice).

Rachel wrote most of the text based on a series of improvisations that we did in English and French. There were several little vignettes, themes joined together around the central idea of English people settling locally. Jean-Louis is a professional actor and he also took on the role of director. Our children also played minor parts. The play ended with a golf lesson and me whacking plastic golf balls over the public and singing Frank Sinatra's "My Way." We included the post office "ca ca" scene accompanied by a song sung as a round.

He sends his poo, All the way to Germany
In a box, in a box , Better get there quick-e-ly before it rots

We did seven performances, all over the Tarn-et-Garonne department and it was very well received. Best of all though, I started to see Jean-Louis as a creative being rather than some sort of villain who'd gone off with my wife.

Not long afterwards, I had a relationship with Carey, an English woman living in Paris. During the first year of knowing Carey we were both surprised to discover that she was pregnant. Although she was a wonderful person and we were very fond of each other I didn't want to start another family in the conventional way as I was 59 by then.

Some months later a baby boy Maxwell was born. I would go up to Paris every six months and over the years we have developed a strong bond of love and friendship. He is a lovely boy and I'm proud to be his father. He also gets on really well with my other children, Leo and Anna. Happily I also have a wonderful relationship with his mother, Carey.

I also had strong support during this time from my family in Scotland and my extended family in London and the children and I made frequent visits to the UK to attend bar mitzvahs, weddings and funerals.

My Son Maxwell, aged eight.

I have five cousins and a sister-in-law, all of us born in 1947 and every five years we have been hosting a birthday party for the whole family in a hotel in Oxford.

There's usually around 140 of us and the festivities last the whole weekend.

I have had many fleeting relationships since Rachel left but nothing that lasted. It was perhaps because Rachel remained such a close confidante and friend, but also because I threw all my energies into the development of La Roane.

I built eight new bedrooms. I realised that the demographic of our guests was changing. The average age is now over fifty and they almost all want single rooms. It often caused problems when people travelling on their own were obliged to share rooms, so I felt it would be better to offer everyone a single room with a very low single supplement charge.

One group of dancers from the south east of England visit La Roane are frequent visitors to La Roane. Their average age is around seventy and these women are a source of inspiration to everyone that meets them. They do what they call circle dancing, mostly folk dances from all over the world, usually dancing in a circle, holding hands. The dances are often meditative but can also be celebratory and jolly.

They are led by Anne Armstrong, a sprightly 83 year old exuding positivity. When she is asked how she is, it is always "splendid!"

Above: With Anne Armstrong, Circle Dancer

Below: Circle Dancing at la Roane

They dance morning, afternoon and evening, with a stop at 6:30 pm to drink a gin and tonic before the evening meal. Their favourite story and one that they re-tell every time they come, is about a canoe trip they made down our local river the Aveyron. The evening before the canoe trip I made a speech, describing exactly how to negotiate the rapids in the river. I explained where to stop for a picnic and where I would be waiting for them at a certain time.

I also described where the canoe trip was to end. Unfortunately they'd had a little more gin than usual and they were not all listening very attentively to my instructions.

The day of the canoe trip was a little bit cold but it was sunny. I went to the picnic spot to wait for them. I waited and waited but nobody turned up. I started to get worried. One of them had recently had a heart attack and I feared for the worst. Remember, these were not young people. What if they had drowned? I left my colleague with the picnic and I started to drive up and down the river looking for them. They were nowhere to be found. By now I was getting frantic. Two hours had passed since they were due to arrive at the picnic spot. Just then I got a phone call from Jane, one of our guests.

Luckily mobile phones had recently become popular.

Above: At the La Roane pool

Below: Morning exercises

She told me that they had gone down the river in couples in seven different canoes, but that the ones in front had gone straight past the picnic spot and straight past the finishing point of the trip. The ones behind had felt obligated to follow so that everyone would stay together. They were now about eight miles further down the river, heading for the Atlantic Ocean.

"Stop right there!" I said. "We are coming to get you."

Most people in the group felt it had been a wonderful adventure, but a few were quite upset and some even traumatised. They had been worried that they might encounter more rapids or dangerous waterfalls. We eventually got everyone back home and I made my apologies for any responsibility that I might have had for the day's outing.

Davy and Janaki have made a number of visits to La Roane to teach yoga. They had been living together for a little before coming to teach their first course. At dinner on the last evening we made one big long celebratory table. Davy told us that he wanted to make an after dinner speech and asked for it to be videoed. This seemed quite normal, but at the end of the meal he got down on his knees and started talking about Janaki being the love of his life and asking for her hand in marriage.

La Roane at dusk.

A very astonished Janaki happily agreed and then the video shows me turning to the girl next to me and saying enthusiastically,

"Jennifer, how about you and me?" to which she responds with a most emphatic:

"No Nigel!"

For me the spirit of community at La Roane has always been most important. The shared joy, inspiration and common purpose brings about transformation and it is a pleasure to witness. A lot of my life's endeavours have been about providing a safe and loving haven for people to come together in harmony and make changes to their lives. Now at the age of 73, (Christ that sounds ancient!) I'm slowly handing over the overall responsibility of La Roane to my wonderful daughter Anna, who is already doing a brilliant job. I will still be involved with the guests which is what I love most but Anna will be in charge and it will her vision and her enthusiasm that will eventually shape the future of La Roane.

With my three elder brothers at a family event.
Left to right, Edward, Donald, Alan and me.
Sadly Edward died in 2010.

FIFTEEN

AYAHUASCA

Iquitos, Peru, 2014

Ayahuasca is a brew made from two plants growing in the jungles of South America, administered in long overnight rituals, usually by a highly experienced shaman. It has been practised since time immemorial in countries such as Peru and Ecuador. Those using this concoction prefer to call it plant medicine and it has become popular in recent years with westerners to cure addictions or to gain insights into our mission in life. Of all the millions of plants in the jungle, how on earth did our ancestors figure out which were the two plants, when mixed in a certain way, could either make you mad as a box of frogs or enable you to meet your maker?

Ayahuasca stimulates the production of a substance called DMT, the same substance that is produced naturally at birth or death. It is also produced by certain types of yogic breathing or very long exposure to darkness. The spirit of ayahuasca is often portrayed as a very wild, old grandmother who will reveal all to you but at the same time is not afraid to smack you hard to help you learn your lesson.

215

I'd read encouraging reports of the experience, so with eager anticipation I flew off to Lima in Peru in January 2014. I had been told by an acquaintance that I should go and work with a certain shaman near the jungle town of Iquitos on the River Amazon. I was impatient to begin and although still slightly jet-lagged I took a flight to Iquitos where I was met by the shaman, Don Pedro. Just as well he came to show me the way because after a long taxi ride and crossing a river in a boat, we had a tortuous four mile trek through the jungle to get to his little settlement. I was a little surprised when he invited me to take part in a ceremony that very evening. I had been eating carefully as advised beforehand, avoiding sugar, salt and alcohol but I was pretty tired and unfocused. I speak good Spanish but Don Pedro's jungle Spanish wasn't easy to understand. I believe that there were three other participants in the ceremony that night but I couldn't see them because it was pitch black and we were told not to talk.

I drank the ayahuasca in one gulp as advised. It tasted horrible. After a few minutes Don Pedro started singing an eerie song called an *Icaros* and making strange percussive sounds. I was sick in a bowl which had been conveniently placed by my mattress. This purging is thought to heal the emotional body as well as the physical. Maybe, but you certainly don't do this for fun! I lay back and had certain visions and insights; nothing dramatic. Soon I went to sleep. The next day I was told to go and rest in my cabin deep in the jungle which seemed to be in the middle of nowhere. The shaman told me not to speak to anyone and simply enjoy the peace and quiet in preparation for the next ceremony which was to take place the following evening. Peace and quiet; what a joke! The jungle is incredibly noisy and I needed earplugs to get any peace at night, what with cicadas, noisy frogs, parrots and howling monkeys. Don Pedro brought me food from time to time but I felt lonely and completely out of my comfort zone.

I turned up for the ceremony the following evening, again in the pitch dark, unable to see anyone else. After a short opening invocation Don Pedro asked,

"Do you want a big dose, Miguel?" I always call myself Miguel in Spanish speaking countries as Nigel is not an easy name to pronounce.

"Sure," I replied. He must have realised that I can handle my ayahuasca, I thought hopefully. He must know exactly what he's doing.

Same procedure; vomiting at the beginning but this time the vomiting was horrific and the visions that went with it even more so. I flew into a complete and utter panic. I was in some other reality where different rules seemed to apply and I just didn't understand the game.

There were demonic visions. I had to get out and leave the ceremony: easier said than done. My body was immobilized but I was so determined to leave that with the help of the shaman's wife I managed to make my exit. She led me to a small cabin, somewhere in the jungle. I had no sense of time or space and as she lay me down I felt relieved.

"Can I leave you now Miguel" she asked, after a few moments.

I thought no, but said yes. Bad move. The horrific visions returned with new force. I tried to get out of the cabin but every time I tried I conjured up six different exits. Utter confusion. I thought if only I could conjure up a pretty girl, that would help. Immediately she appeared but instead of being pleased I was terrified. I thought I was going mad and wondered if I'd ever be normal. Somehow I managed to exit the cabin and I lay on the ground. I vomited fiercely and I remember the vomit making strange patterns. I yelled and cried for help. Nobody came. I must have stayed a few minutes like this but I lost all track of time. It was hell.

Eventually the shaman's son came and helped me back into the cabin. He got me to breathe and to pray and eventually the demonic visions started to fade. He took me on the long walk back to my isolated cabin to rest. I should have gone back to the others. We sat together for a while and then he asked if he could go. Again I should have said no but I said yes. I was still between worlds and I kept seeing a weird ghost outside my cabin. Soon my candle went out, then the battery of my torch expired and I was in the dark with all the horrific jungle noises and the scary ghost. It was a long and unpleasant night and I had almost no sleep. The next day I packed and grabbed my suitcase, desperate to get away as quickly as possible. Don Pedro was nowhere to be seen.

Now I can tell you, should it ever happen to you, that Iquitos is the worst place in the world to recover from an ayahuasca ceremony. Scooter taxis were buzzing around like angry hornets, tooting their horns incessantly. I managed to find a quiet hotel away from the noise but it had just been built and I think I was the only customer. I was very lonely. I didn't have a mobile phone and I felt scared being in the room alone that evening. However I survived and two days later I flew via Lima to Cusco and made my way through the Sacred Valley to Machu Picchu, a 15th century Inca citadel located at an altitude of 8,000 feet in the foothills of the Andes. Unfortunately I was still feeling incredibly sensitive and all the wonders of that very special place were lost on me. I found it difficult to be outgoing and sociable. I was like a wounded soldier and so I returned to the town of Cusco.

Wandering around the town for a few hours I eventually came across a shop called Magic Hands. I was greeted by the friendly owner Jesus who gave me a big hug.

"I've been waiting for you," he said.

At last, I thought, someone who knows me and understands me. He sold artifacts made with crystals to ward off evil spirits and invoke good energies. He was utterly charming. Jesus showed me testimonials written by Americans, some of them well-known and he advised me to look up his credentials on the internet. I was so happy to have the comfort of a friend and didn't feel the need to investigate further. He was someone who could listen to my tale of woe with sympathy. He wanted to sell me a special protective life changing necklace for what he said was the bargain price of only US$ 250.

"I'll go to the ATM and bring it tomorrow," I told him.

"No problem," he said. "I have my car right outside and I will take you there right now."

I was slightly surprised that he was so eager to make the transaction, but I paid him and went home with the necklace, feeling calmer and confident that I was being protected.

Some days later out of interest I googled Magic Hands. I seemed to remember that he had met Shirley MacLaine, a hero of mine. The first thing I saw was, "Don't go to Magic Hands because Jesus is a con-artist." Several people gave this feedback and of course I felt incredibly stupid. When I returned to the shop to ask for a refund, Jesus was nowhere to be found and his shop seemed to be closed. And so I returned to Lima for want of a better option.

In Lima I was robbed twice, first by a taxi driver sitting next to me and then on a bus by a little boy, sitting in the next seat. Twice I got taken in by hard luck stories and gave away money. It was as if in my weakened state of being, I was a sitting duck for every hustler on the lookout for easy money. There were not huge sums of money, but I am a seasoned traveller and this didn't make me feel good.

I'm losing the plot, I thought. I toyed with the idea of going home but airfares were exorbitantly expensive. I had been in contact with my dear ex-wife Rachel. I told her I was a bit lost and not sure what to do next. She did a lot of research and told me the next day to go to the Hare Krishna community north of Lima called Eco Truly. I knew I could never belong to the Hare Krishna sect, but it seemed like a good place to rest and recuperate. It was right beside a beautiful, clear, pristine beach. At least it was clear until the weekend when thousands of holiday makers would head north from Lima to escape the perpetual cloud hanging over the city. By Monday morning they'd all gone home and the place looked like a bomb site with cans of beer and plastic rubbish everywhere. A huge team of workers arrived for the cleanup and by mid day it was in tip top shape again. Strange way to go about things, but at least our beach remained clean during weekdays.

The Hare Krishna community was indeed a great place to recover and get over the trauma of the last few weeks. We chanted the Hare Krishna mantra daily and I spent time working in the garden and in the kitchen. I swam in the sea and did yoga on the beach.

Some weeks later I returned to France a little bit worse for wear but certainly a lot better than I had been after my misadventure in Iquitos two months previously. Never again, I thought.

La Gomera, Canary Islands, 2017

Three years later I was again seeking to escape winter in France and I ended up on the little island of La Gomera, a short boat trip from Tenerife in the Canary Islands. Three weeks into my stay there was a hippie market taking place and I overheard a conversation about an ayahuasca ceremony the coming weekend. I pricked up my ears. After my Peruvian experience I'd sworn that I'd never touch the stuff again.

But I had begun to think as the years passed that I had perhaps some unfinished business with the plant. What was it trying to tell me? Where did these frightful, demonic visions come from? I couldn't trace them easily to this life. I had had a pleasant childhood with no obvious traumas and I didn't suffer from nightmares. Were these visions real? Now that I had some experience of the plant, perhaps I could just observe the visions and they would surely disappear.

I approached the organiser of the group, a German woman. I didn't have a particularly good connection with her. She seemed stressed and in a hurry but when she told me that it was the last place available that seemed like a good omen and I booked myself in for the ceremony the following day. The ceremony which was illegal in Spain was on the other side of the island in a remote, rather cold and windy country house. We were a group of thirteen, mostly German with two or three Spanish. We had a sharing circle to begin the ceremony where all thirteen of us talked briefly about why we had come. This was a big improvement on my Peruvian experience, but sadly I still felt little sense of rapport with the shaman. After taking the drink I had the usual horrendous vomiting and then horror of horrors, the same dreadfully scary visions. I remember feeling very annoyed with myself. I'd put myself in danger, even though I'd vowed not to. I'd done it again, I thought.

I staggered out of the group into the open in abject misery, thinking things would be better outside. They got worse; more demonic visions of grotesque creatures. Finally the Spanish assistant to the shaman came to help me. Sometimes she would appear to turn into a metal machine, but she was nevertheless helpful. She eventually persuaded me to come back into the circle. I remember visions of ugly gigantic maggots and faeces. Eventually it all quietened down and I sang a song or two to the group and that seemed to help me a lot. Soon after we all went off to sleep. We had quite a convivial atmosphere the next morning and we had a short discussion about our experiences. I returned to my hotel, feeling lighter and very positive. I was happy to have survived the experience and it was a huge improvement compared with my Peruvian experience but I remember feeling pretty sure that I would never do it again.

Lake Atitlan, Guatemala, 2020

I'm now in Guatemala by Lake Atitlan in the midst of the Corona outbreak. Here you can find any kind of plant medicine available, for example San Pedro and peyote (both cactus based) and of course ayahuasca. I had now recovered from my previous encounters with the plant but I wasn't keen to repeat the experience.

A few weeks into my stay I came across a Mexican shaman called Rodrigo whom I trusted. He was offering two plant medicines which worked very well together, kambo and bufo. A kambo cleanse is a purge using skin poisons of the kambo frog from the Amazon jungle which according to Rodrigo was humanely extracted. He told us that kambo is not hallucinogenic but that it is an excellent plant to take before taking bufo. After a short ceremony he administered the plant via five abrasions in a row that he made on my left arm. Ha, I thought; I've got a sort of tattoo just like everyone else! The experience was horrific; vomiting and then diarrhoea. Normally I would have been embarrassed by this as there were several others doing the ceremony but that seemed to be the least of my worries. Eventually I recovered, glad that it was over. Rodrigo assured me that my body was now in a far better state to receive bufo in a couple of days' time.

Bufo is a poison which comes from a special type of toad found in the Mexican desert. It's known sometimes as the grandson of ayahuasca. Its effect is less dramatic and lasts only for about thirty minutes. However like ayahuasca, bufo produces the chemical DMT, the most powerful psychedelic of all, said to stimulate the pituitary gland and facilitate contact with other realities. Rodrigo asked me to state my intentions for the experience and I told him that I wanted to be more loving and to open my heart. He blew smoke made from the bufo up my nostrils and the effect was almost instantaneous. I felt an opening of the heart, I felt love for all humanity and it seemed that my head had lit up. It was very short but it was a fantastic experience and I had no ill effects afterwards.

I started to feel less scared of ayahuasca. I was doing 2 hrs of yoga every morning with the other residents in our little hotel. In addition Samuel, my German house mate, was teaching me Wim Hof breathing. This is a type of forceful inhalation followed by retention after breathing out. Combined with cold showers and yoga it can also produce DMT in the body. I was feeling healthy and content, happier than I'd been for many years. However, I was in no hurry to take ayahuasca. There were plenty of opportunities but nothing felt quite right.

Some three months after being here, Samuel arrived back at the hotel, telling me excitedly that he had been on a wonderfully restorative ayahuasca journey with a young couple, Mitsu from Peru and Vero from Germany. I was intrigued, but this time I wanted to make sure that I could trust and relate to the shaman. I met them on a couple of occasions and they turned out to be beautiful souls whom I felt closely connected to. I was particularly drawn to Mitsu. He had had a difficult background but now his smiling face seemed to glow with happiness and wellbeing. I signed up for the ceremony which was to take place in a couple of days.

When the big day arrived we made our way up to a healing centre in the mountains above San Marcos. It was all highly illegal as we were not supposed to have large gatherings because of Corona virus and so we went up in groups of two or three.

There were thirteen of us in the group plus Mitsu, Vero and a young Guatemalan Nero who was in charge of the fire. They were a wonderful group of people. I was by some thirty years the oldest in the group, but I felt humbled by the wisdom and sincerity of these young people.

The ceremony began at 4 p.m. We breathed in rapé, a derivative of the tobacco plant, up our noses to elevate the spirit and prepare us for the next stage. We then took a plant called yopo which contains the chemical DMT and produces hallucinations, but is taken principally to clean the body and prepare it as a vehicle for ayahuasca. It was accompanied with a half dosage of ayahuasca.

Coloured patterns appeared in my head, accompanied by horrendous vomiting. Why do I do this? I thought to myself. I'm so crazy! After about forty minutes the worst effects passed.

We were ready for a full glass of ayahuasca. I thought I was well prepared this time but the spirit of ayahuasca showed no sympathy for me. It was as if I'd taken on the pain of the whole world. I was crying and weeping to some sort of angry black Earth Mother for the sins of slavery. The more scared I became, the more the noise in my ears seemed to increase in volume. I was crying and vomiting and apparently making a great deal of noise because Mitsu came and told me to quieten down as I was upsetting the others. I apologised profusely. I tried to lie down. I wanted to curl up and die but Mitsu grabbed me and squeezed me tight.

"*Eres guerrero*, You're a warrior!" he said. "*Eres yogi, respire, respire*! You're a yogi, breathe, breathe!"

And so I did. Miraculously the horrific vision disappeared. I have never felt such gratitude. I went back to my place in the room.

After a few minutes Mitsu asked if anyone wanted to sing some songs and delighted, I volunteered and sang my heart out, accompanying myself with the guitar for thirty minutes. It felt like I was giving something back to the group because I had felt their love and support during my ordeal. The worst was over but the night was long. We sat around the fire, sometimes singing, sometimes meditating, until at last dawn broke. What a relief! We talked, we hugged and we ate breakfast. It felt as if we'd all been on a very long journey for about a week. So many of our prayers in the ceremony had been for the healing of our world which seemed to be in such crisis. Just as we were completing the closing ceremony, a patch of blue sky appeared from nowhere directly above us and it seemed like a blessing for our group.

I took ayahuasca this last time to try to understand why my experiences with the plant are so much more powerful than anyone else's. It seems to me that I am what is called an empath, someone who is very sensitive to the emotions of others. When I see people cry, I cry. When they laugh, I laugh. I realise that my task is to be compassionate but at the same time have a certain detachment from the emotions of others. Whether these emotions that provoke the horrific visions come from the people around me, my ancestors or the pain of the whole world is probably something I will never know for sure but I feel that they do not come directly from this present life.

Since that experience I have felt more inspired, more loving and more creative than ever before.

I am at peace with myself and feel no need whatsoever to take ayahuasca again.

SIXTEEN
BEING HAPPY

I strongly believe that we are so much more than we think we are. We get into certain daily routines; we might become engrossed in the media and the business of life and we forget that we are filled with infinite potential. At various times in my life I witnessed extraordinary things which transformed the way I saw the world. I remember seeing a fakir in India lie on a bed of nails and another one having concrete slabs smashed over his chest. I witnessed Swami Gitananda slow his heart rate down to three beats per minute. I have seen miracles of manifestation with gurus such as Sai Baba and Premananda which I have described earlier. All these seeming miracles were fascinating for a young man in search of his path in life. After a while however I wanted more. I craved a direct experience of the miraculous rather than relying on someone else to perform miracles.

About fifteen years ago I organized a fire walking ceremony at La Roane which was run by a couple of women from Italy, Liliana and Sienna. About fifteen local people turned up. We talked together as a group and we were asked to state our intentions for the afternoon. We chanted mantras or sacred sounds to bring the group together and to create a sacred atmosphere in the room.

The next exercise was to put a wooden arrow pointing inwards onto our sternums, then pull the arrow towards us and finally to break it. Normally this would have been impossible without causing serious damage but everyone seemed to manage it quite easily. We were building up trust in our abilities. Then we paired up and we placed fairly heavy metal bars between our foreheads. The couple would press the bar with their heads until it bent. Not everyone managed it but it was impressive nevertheless.

I had collected chestnut wood for the fire to produce a strong heat. The fire had been burning away whilst we were doing our preparatory rituals but by the time we had finished it had almost gone out. Liliana raked the embers which were still glowing red. We surrounded the fire in a circle in a spirit of love and harmony. Liliana and Sienna walked slowly and confidently across the three meters of embers with no ill effects whatsoever and the rest of us followed on one by one. Many of us did it several times over. It was astonishing. We should have been severely burned. Some of us had tiny little red marks on the soles of our feet but after soaking them in water for a few minutes all was well. I did another fire ceremony a few months later with similar results. It's an excellent team building exercise but also a very important lesson in what is possible.

One of the strangest things I've ever witnessed happened in Mexico in 2016. My daughter Anna was doing a one year course at the University of Guadalajara as part of her degree at Toulouse University and I went there to spend three months with her. At one point we met a lovely woman called Yolanda who claimed that we could all see even when blindfolded. Intrigued but rather skeptical, Anna and I signed up for the course she was organising the following weekend.

There were six of us participating plus Yolanda and Maria who was the person in charge. We held hands, did some breathing exercises and tried in a moment of silence to connect with our divine essence. We then paired up and sat on chairs back to back. We were given a piece of paper with six symbols, circles, squares, triangles and the like and we were asked to telepathically send one of the symbols to our partners. We would tell our partner when we were sending it and they would then record it. This was done six times. Anna and I got both well above average results with the other participants but working together the results were even more convincing. We did other similar exercises over the course of the afternoon, the object being to get us to believe in our abilities.

The following exercise, the highlight of the afternoon was done one by one. Three of us including Anna and I were to work with Yolanda and the other three with Maria. I volunteered to go first and the other two were sent out of the room. Yolanda asked me to start reading a magazine full of text and glossy pictures. She slowly started to wrap a bandage quite tightly around my face as I continued reading. After a while I couldn't see anything.

"Look for the hole in the bandage," she said. I couldn't see any hole.

"Keep looking," she continued.

Eventually I found the hole and started reading and describing the pictures. The hole then disappeared but I found it a second time. Sometimes it was there and sometimes it disappeared. My eyes had been completely covered and there was no hole and yet I had been able to see.

I watched as Anna then tried. The bandage definitely covered every part of her eyes so that she looked like the Michelin Man. It would have been utterly impossible for her to see through the bandages. She had similar results to me as did the other participants.

My daughter Anna, my granddaughter Lucia and me

Yolanda explained that we can use our third eye which is situated between the physical eyes to see things intuitively. It was altogether remarkable. She went on to say that we could practice this technique and very soon we would have a continuous image of what we were seeing.

She told us that she also runs more advanced courses so that you can read even when the text is held behind you. She said that the technique is used to develop the third eye and our powers of intuition.

The main thing I learned is that we have an enormous ability to go way beyond what is normally thought possible. But do these things actually help you become happier? It's certainly helpful to have a regular meditation and yoga habit, and techniques such as fire walking or seeing whilst blindfolded can indeed help us to push the boundaries of what we can achieve. I remember in the 1980's setting up Cortijo Romero and using creative visualisation techniques. These techniques really work.

However, as I got older I started to realise that we don't always know what is best for us. The hardest lesson in my life has been to let go and surrender to the process of life. I would go to extremes in yoga and meditation for example, desperate for results and not a lot happened.

With age I realise that I often tried too hard. It's important to go with the flow and not become obsessed about results.

I love the Serenity Prayer.

Grant me the serenity to accept the things I cannot change,
The courage to change the things I can
And the wisdom to know the difference.

But how to find out what is our path? When to change things and when to surrender? What are the best techniques to use? How should I live my life? I have spent almost fifty years reading self help books and I know the limitations of someone writing about great yoga techniques, meditations or whatever and expecting them to bring about huge changes in other people's lives. They may work for a while, maybe even longer, but we all have such individual paths to walk and we all have to find our own way, using whatever techniques are appropriate. I think that we are guided along throughout our lives and that we have guardian angels or some sort of unseen helpers. When we go off track a little, they are there to help us if we just ask, as I've seen so many times in my life. So yes, we have to be open to help from the unseen, to look for omens and synchronicity in dreams, in nature and in our daily encounters. The more open we are, the more guidance we will receive.

All I can do is to talk about the things that have helped me to find peace in *my* life. If I were to select only one thing I would say that it would be the power of laughter. The healing power of laughter has been well documented. There was the groundbreaking book in the 1970's by the American journalist Norman Cousins "Anatomy of an Illness" in which he overcomes the killer disease ankylosing spondylitis through laughter.

The doctors had given him a one in 500 chance of survival and he decided to spend his last few months laughing. He watched Candid Camera, Marx Brothers films and the like and his friends took turns to come and tell him funny stories. Nobody was allowed in his hospital room unless they were going to cheer him up. He found that ten minutes of genuine belly laughter could relieve his intense pain for one hour. Cousins had hit upon a fundamental truth which has been confirmed countless times in the laboratory. Laughter produces feel-good chemicals in the brain called endorphins and is excellent for health and social bonding.

I remember as a youngster in my 20's that I'd always been drawn to organising laughter games. Whenever I was stoned I always tried to be amusing and to get people to join in the fun. I devised all sorts of silly games that could be played at parties. I would rarely repeat them. The humour was in the spontaneity.

As I got older and more confident I learned to do this without artificial stimulants.

Rasta Man

Around twenty years ago I started to incorporate these techniques into my yoga and Chi Kung classes. Yoga and Chi Kung can be quite serious, but I found that getting people to laugh at the beginning of the class promoted group harmony and usually helped bring people into the present moment.

When I was in India in 2006 doing an Ayurvedic retreat, I heard of a doctor from Mumbai, Dr. Kataria who taught a series of laughter exercises that he called Laughter Yoga. I didn't feel drawn to him at the time, not wanting to do a series of set exercises and couldn't imagine people really sticking to them unless they were genuinely funny. I continued doing my laughter exercises over the following years much as before.

About ten years later I learned that Dr. Kataria, now world famous and the inspiration for thousands of Laughter Yoga Clubs all over the world, was heading a Laughter Conference in Paris. My friend Amaryllis was very keen for me to accompany her so we went together on the train. There were about 300 people at the conference from all over the world. It was held in a big residential complex just outside Paris. At any time of the day there was a large choice of workshops to attend, all of them on the theme of laughter. Mostly it was people who had been trained by Dr. Kataria going through a series of techniques. After every exercise we would clap our hands and say "ha ha ha, ho ho hi!"

I found it irritating even though it had been proven clinically that even if you fake laughter, the effects are just as beneficial.

My attitude all depended on the group leader. There were some excellent group leaders and if that person were a natural clown then the sessions would be wonderful, but if they were just going through a list of exercises it did nothing for me.

Dr. Kataria was interesting. He was a charismatic teacher and very good at explaining the medical benefits of laughter and how to go about setting up Laughter Clubs. Even though he wasn't particularly funny, he could hold the attention of three-hundreed people at the conference and inspire them to take laughter seriously. There was another side to him that I liked. He was a spiritual man and devoted to yoga. In the morning he would lead mantra chanting. All three-hundreed of us would take deep breaths and on the exhalation chant together certain vowel sounds. It was a magical way to start the day.

Most of the people there had a lot of experience of laughter therapy. They laughed easily and the result at the end of the course was a wonderful sense of cohesion, harmony and love. I remember the journey home on the train with Amaryllis. We couldn't stop laughing. Eventually we went to the special compartment for children and we continued laughing there until a slightly disgruntled passenger told us that she'd come to this compartment to get away from us.

I wanted more and I signed up to attend another Laughter Conference in Madrid the following weekend. Dr. Kataria had gone off to the USA, but it was led by a very nice man from Grenada called Javier. This time there were only sixty people, but I really enjoyed myself. The Spanish laugh very easily and there was a very convivial atmosphere. Over the course of the weekend I had to learn thirty different techniques advocated by Dr. Kataria, to encourage people to laugh and I was given a Laughter Facilitator's certificate to lead groups.

Later that year I started running my own laughter groups in a community hall near where I lived in France. I was surprised to find that some of the exercises that I had learned in Madrid were quite useful, especially to start off the laughter process. I would use one or two of the techniques to generate a festive atmosphere. The fun really started though when I would improvise with the group, using whatever stimulation or prop that was being offered.

I did it for free which was both bad and good. People would sometimes be loathe to venture out when they were feeling bad on a cold winter's evening and if they hadn't paid for a term of classes they were less motivated to come.

It was a diverse group of people. The pillar of the group was Brigitte. She had a resounding laugh and when she burst into fits of giggles, it had a viral effect on all the others and we would all end up in fits of laughter. I usually tried to calm them down at the end of the session with various kinds of yogic breathing. Through the shared laughter and madness of these sessions, deep bonds of friendship were created within the group.

The purpose of group laughter is to encourage laughter in your daily life. We always have the ability to smile or laugh. You can just start by changing the shape of your mouth and little by little through repetition it becomes a habit. I try never to start the day without laughing at myself in the mirror and telling myself what a fine fellow I am!

The following year I went to a Laughter Yoga Conference in the UK. The highlight for me was not the laughter but an evening of Scottish country dancing, complete with accordion, violin, banjo and a caller, a woman trained to yell out the instructions. Scottish country dancing is a fantastic way to break the ice. It's very physical, you swing your partners all over the place and usually nobody takes it too seriously. I make sure to include it in my laughter yoga sessions.

That winter I decided to go to Bangalore, India to do a ten day course with Dr. Kataria. I was curious to know what I could learn from him. It wasn't an easy course for him to lead. Half the students were Japanese and they used an interpreter as they didn't speak English. They tended to act as a group and didn't seem to go for spontaneous expression. I was very impressed with Dr. Kataria. As the standard bearer for laughter yoga he has to always show a laughing face when in public. In addition he is the head of a huge organisation. He explained that he keeps himself sane with a daily dose of laughter, usually about thirty minutes but also, most importantly, deep yogic relaxation.

I didn't learn any new techniques but I left with a deep conviction of the importance of laughter. Not only have I tried to cultivate the habit of laughing at myself in the mirror each morning but at various times in the day, if I catch myself being miserable or blaming others, I just laugh or smile. Incidentally, with all these masks which we have to wear during the Corona virus scare, if you are inhibited about laughing or smiling in public, you can always do it behind your mask. I have two masks that coordinate well with the different colours of clothes that I wear here in San Marcos. On one of them I got the tailor to add a very realistic flesh coloured nose which seems to confuse the local police.

Any tool that can change our energy and bring us back to the present moment is helpful. Something that I discovered three months ago is the Wim Hof breathing technique. It's almost the same as the bellows breath or *bhastrika* which I learned with Swami Gitananda in India nearly fifty years ago. The breathing is done lying down and with a long retention after the out breath to oxygenate the blood cells. The effect is to increase energy levels and boost the immune system.

Wim, also known as the Ice Man, because of his body's tolerance of extreme temperatures, also recommends cold showers and cold water immersion. This is done in stages, so as not to shock the body too much. He seems to spend half his time in laboratories, astounding scientists with his feats. For example, several thousand human guinea pigs were injected with e coli bacteria and without exceptions showed symptoms of the disease (incidentally they were all well paid for the pleasure!).

Wim Hof was then injected with the same bacteria but showed no symptoms of disease.

"That's because you're special, you're the Ice Man," argued the scientists.

"No," he replied. "Give me a team of volunteers and within four days I'll train them to do the same."

He led his volunteers up some freezing cold mountains in Poland where they stayed for four days and then they went home and practiced breathing exercises for six days. The volunteers were then able to astound the scientists with their resistance to e coli.

The other benefit of Wim Hof breathing is that it is a wonderful prelude to meditation. After doing this breathing technique, simply sitting peacefully gives mental clarity and makes us more receptive to new ideas. This has been a huge help to me because I've never found meditation to be easy.

Starting and maintaining this practice requires a certain discipline but for the moment I love doing it. The moment I don't enjoy it or start to get obsessive about it I will find something equally or even more inspiring to keep me on the path. Again we are faced with the question posed by the Serenity Prayer of when to be self disciplined and when to let go and surrender.

Another of my passions is singing. More recently I have become a fan of gospel music after attending a couple of gospel weekends run by a woman from Haiti and a man from Nigeria. What voices! They were so tiny in stature. Where did their immense voices come from? I loved the fact that we could all dance around spontaneously, clap our hands and really feel the music which was such a far cry from standard church music. The songs were sung with such love and sincerity and without any feeling of one up manship vis-a-vis other religions that I didn't even mind singing about Jesus being my saviour.

The group leaders Didi and Emanuel told me that in their cultures they had always been encouraged to sing, that people would just start singing spontaneously without embarrassment. I've come to realise that for the voice to flow easily we have to be uninhibited. Over the years, I have led around fifty one week courses and singing is always an important part of these courses. I'm not really a singing teacher, but I do know how to get people to lose their inhibitions by moving, breathing and laughing. Time and time again it has proven that this can produce amazing results.

One of the very best things for me about being older is that I no longer want to have sex with every beautiful woman I see. This gives me a huge amount of freedom. Young women, rightly or wrongly tend not to see men of my age as predators or as a threat. We are valued more for our empathy and sensitivity. When I first arrived in San Marcos I met a woman on a yoga retreat. After the retreat she returned to the USA and we would talk regularly on the phone. When I tentatively broached the subject over the phone of whether we might become more intimate, she replied that she really valued our friendship, but that she would rather stay that way, just good friends. Earlier in my life I would gradually have lost interest in this friendship, but that night it occurred to me that at the end of my life I would rather be considered a loving and kind friend than someone with sex appeal.

I have been sharing with you some of the things which keep me sane and inspired about being alive. More generally, growing older has given me a greater freedom from the need to strive and compete and worry about what people might think of me. I do things because I want to do them, rather than having to. I look at the media less, I make fewer appointments and I seem to have more time and less stress. I am more able to surrender to the process of life rather than always trying to make things happen. Best of all I have three wonderful children whom I adore. I also have a gorgeous two year old granddaughter to play with and she thinks I'm very funny! Most importantly I have no regrets. I have been blessed in this life to have been able to do whatever has taken my fancy and I give thanks to everyone that made this possible.

I have come to understand how everything that happens is a sort of gift. If there hadn't been the seeds of discontent within me I would never have started my wanderings.

At La Roane

Had I not taken LSD at a crucial time in my life and tasted another version of reality, I might not have been so ardent in my quest to wake up and search new horizons. Yes, even Rachel leaving me, which was the biggest blow of my life, has turned out to be a great gift and has enabled us both to be more of what we were meant to be and at the same time continue to be the best of friends.

To summarise, let me say that it's important to cultivate good habits such as laughter, breathing exercises and singing, all of which help us to come into the present moment.

At the same time we have to seek out the company of those that will inspire us on our path. With gratitude and with love we open ourselves to the Divine.

I would like to conclude by encouraging everyone to write their autobiography. I didn't think there was much to tell but once I started, the stories came pouring out and I couldn't stop. The paradox is that we are so insignificant in the great scheme of things and at the same time so powerful. The self reflection involved in writing our stories helps us to see our place in the world.

And finally, a poem which has greatly inspired me. It's by the 13th century Persian mystic Rumi called the *Guest House* which is about being with whatever life brings us, whether it comes in the form of great joy or great difficulty.

This being human is a guest house

Each day a new arrival.
A joy, a depression, a meanness
Some momentary awareness comes
As an unexpected visitor
Welcome and entertain them all!
Even if they are a cloud of sorrows
Who violently sweep your house empty of its furniture
Still, treat each guest honourably.
He may be clearing you out for some new delight
The dark thought, the shame, the malice
Meet them at the door laughing
And invite them in
Be grateful for whatever comes
Because each has been sent as a guide from beyond

ACKNOWLEDGEMENTS

My thanks to Luke Maguire Armstrong for his helpful suggestions, to Tina Dragon for typing the manuscripts, to Dorota Reising and cousin Terry for editing the text and to my wonderful publisher Sabrina Mesko of Arnica Press.

Finally thanks to family and friends, teachers and mentors for their love, support and encouragement throughout the years.

ABOUT THE AUTHOR

Nigel Shamash was born and educated in Scotland, the fourth son of Jews from Baghdad in Iraq. He has had a varied career as a banker in South America, Senior lecturer in Business Studies at Portsmouth Polytechnic and a yoga teacher and masseur in Australia. His interest in self development and mysticism led to twelve visits to the Indian subcontinent and a sojourn through California in 1973, staying in alternative communities. He has founded two highly successful holiday centres, Cortijo Romero in Spain and La Roane near Toulouse in south west France, where he currently resides. He runs courses based on themes of yoga, song and laughter in various parts of the world.

For information about La Roane
and courses run by Nigel
Visit his website at:

www.NigelShamash.com

For information about Cortijo Romero:
www.cortijo-romero.co.uk

Printed in Great Britain
by Amazon

64230658R00147